10 Things We Should Teach You In High School and Usually Don't

Pete Herr

Published by:
The Creative Buffalo
17 Waltham Ave.
Lancaster, NY 14086

This book is available for special discounts for bulk purchases for sales
promotions or premiums. For more information email
books@peteherrsuccess.com

ISBN: 0692281835
ISBN-13: 978-0692281833

Library of Congress number applied for.

Cover design by Brittany Carleton

Author photo by David R. Janson

DEDICATION

This book is dedicated to my family. Linda, Adam and Rebecca. I am nothing without you.

And to the many students I have had along the way. What I have learned from you is immeasurable.

CONTENTS

ACKNOWLEDGEMENTS

When I sat down to write this book, I really had no idea what I was in for. I figured I would just pump it out, it'd be perfect, publishers would fall all over themselves to get me to sign with them and then the money would just fall from the sky. I had no idea that it would take over two years to get it done and that the work involved in getting a publisher or agent to even look at your book takes more time than actually writing the book.

There were multiple times along the way that I was just going to give the thing up. Writing a book was, after all, just something I wanted to cross off my bucket list. I'm not sure exactly when it happened, but at some point, I realized that I had something important to say, to parents and teachers and people of all ages who were looking to have a few more good tools in their bag as they looked for their version of success.

It wasn't me or the words I wrote that made me realize that this project had merit. It was my family, friends , and even a few perfect strangers, who nodded and smiled as I told them about it, or who asked questions that I hadn't thought of. Without all of the people around me, this book never would have been realized. So, thanks to all who inspired me, with the conversations, notes, emails, comments on my Facebook wall and any of the other countless affirmations along the way.

I also need to thank these people specifically. This book is a better book because of them.

My wife, Linda and my son Adam - You are the foundation on which I am built. I would not have survived our darkest moments without you. I also would not have persevered and completed this book without you. It would have ended up like painting the ugly garage door. We'll get to it next summer.

To my friends, from different phases of my life that took the time to read the first, sloppy, choppy draft of this book, and offer feedback and corrections. I know that was a time commitment and I truly appreciate it. Thank you Kara & Ryan Bowers, Joe Mineo, Ed Hokaj, Mary Alice Chase, Betsy Durant, Matt Walter, and Steve Naramore.

To two women, fellow authors and good friends, who really dug in with red pens and did extensive editing on the book. When I first looked at the volume of corrections and suggestions, I was certain that this book was a flop. My appreciation for the care you took in pushing me towards a book that people can read is beyond words. A big thank you to Christina Abt and Kate Sciandra.

To Dr. Frank Wood, who guided me through some of the things I wanted to say about the psychology of the human mind.

To my former student, and now colleague, Mark Guay, who agreed to write the foreword to this book with only a "I'd be honored" and "Give me a deadline". As a student, Mark challenged me to be better in the classroom. As a teacher, he is involved in some great initiatives, and challenging his students to be excellent.

To Mike Powers, marketing guy extraordinaire, who never said no when I asked for his thoughts on any aspect of the book.

To Paul Meyerhofer, who jumped in to help me with

my formatting problems.

To John Manzella, who spent quite a bit of time on the phone one day talking me through the ins and outs of publishing a book. I actually took the step because of the confidence I gained from that conversation. I've never met him in person, and he spent the time anyway. The world needs more people like John.

Finally, to the following teachers that I have either had as a student, or have worked with, in one capacity or another, over the years. All good teachers share one trait; they see the value in students and truly enjoy them. The following teachers saw value in me and they continue to inspire me to do the same: Herb Bosch, Mike McCadden, Lenny Pappas, Dr. Steve Reynolds and Jenny Guthrie. The following teachers are among the best I have ever worked with, because they understand that the relationship between teacher and student is based on a mutual respect: Lynn Leonard, Robert Mihelbergel, Rebecca Kranz, Keith Junik and Heather Ruhland. Thanks to all of those teachers for making me a better one.

FOREWORD

I stood two feet planted firm, shoulder width apart, chest back ready to belt out my first note. With a smirk, I sang my heart out completely aware that I chose the *uncensored* version of the musical number I sang as the lead in the high school musical last year. Let's just say that the song involved a number of sexual references completely inappropriate for the small private Catholic school I attended and far too inappropriate for the ears of my dance choreographer, a woman I admired like a grandmother.

I walked away smiling like a little James Dean -- rebellious in a small way, and completely ignorant of the stupidity in my actions.

The next morning I heard my name buzz through the loudspeaker and I walked into Pete Herr's office. There stood a man I deeply admired, not only for his knowledge, wit, and the charisma he shared as my teacher and director in the school play, but also as a surrogate father figure who shared his deep thoughts on life and tips to succeed -- many of the tips he now shares with you in this book.

In just one sentence, Pete called to attention all that I wasn't doing: "What were you thinking?" he asked. "Just, what were you thinking?"

And here's the thing…I wasn't. **I was never taught to.** Sure, I could choose a witty adjective to modify a noun, could describe the events that led to World War II, and could identify a halite rock (HINT: you lick it). But ask me to synthesize my interests and knowledge base to create meaningful work and I'd be lost. Huh? Is this going to be on the test?

Pete taught me many invaluable lessons over the years I spent under his tutelage. Simple habits like goal setting and learning from role models turned out to be not so simple. And so Pete showed me how to break it down. When it came time to choose a career for my life, he sat me down for another father-like speech and helped me look deep within my heart and listen to my gut. He shared a few of his stories which in turn helped motivate me to ask more from myself and to live remarkably.

Chances are you were also part of this factory-based school system and your children are being pushed along the assembly belt as they punch in and punch out of school when the bell rings. This worked well when we lived in the Industrial Age and needed high-quality workers to fill the factories, but the world today requires students to learn how to think conceptually and connect digitally all while digging deep within themselves to find what truly drives them to do meaningful work that goes beyond a paycheck.

Hopefully you had a teacher like Pete Herr and your children do as well. If not, luckily you now have this book in your hands.

In *10 Things We Should Teach You in High School, and Usually Don't*, Pete Herr lays out all of the secrets he shared with me as his student and continues to shares with you.

Who is this book for?

- The parents who want their child to be prepared to enter the new conceptual economy, one that no longer asks students to punch in and punch out, but rather think conceptually and connect globally.

- The entrepreneurial student who wants more and doesn't want to wait till graduation to get started on living a remarkable life.

- The mid-career professional with a quarter-life crisis who finds himself in the grocery store, waiting in the long line to buy food for dinner, to wait in the traffic on the ride home, to then rise up by the alarm day after day and wonders, "Why am I not happy?"

Pick it up, read it, then share it with someone you love. And please, share your story with me on how Pete Herr has helped get you started on living the life you want to live.

To living remarkably,

Mark W. Guay
@markwguay
mark@markwguay.com

INTRODUCTION

Around a decade ago, I had a high school Leadership Class jammed down my throat. We had a new principal and he wanted to bring all of the things that had been successful at his old school to our school. I really wanted nothing to do with it. In retrospect, I was kind of stubborn and kind of dumb. Why not incorporate ideas that were tried, tested and successful? Also, in retrospect, it turned out to be one of the best things to ever happen to me. It's become my signature course over the years. Amazing how that works.

The best thing about teaching a leadership course is that every time I teach it, it is a completely different class. The kids are always bringing new insights from their different life experiences. The world always offers new examples through a constantly changing geopolitical soap opera, or through the bizarre behaviors of our celebrities. Regardless of where the material comes from, there is no shortage of behaviors to model, or to avoid.

Working on this class for as long as I have has given me some really great opportunities, as well. I have gotten to read inspiring books by many of the greatest personal and professional leadership experts. My journey started with the classic "The Seven Habits of Highly Effective People" by Dr. Stephen R. Covey, and has gone on to include John C. Maxwell, Erik Qualman, Tim Ferris, Carrie Wilkerson, Tony Robbins, Napoleon Hill, Brandon Burchard and many others.

My continuing studies would often bring the revelation, "We should definitely teach that in high school so our kids have that skill for the rest of their lives." Eventually, I made a list, and I made sure to include them in my leadership class curriculum. There are so many things I wish I had learned when I was 16 or 17 years old. They would have been game changers in my life. Just because you didn't learn these lessons when you were in high school doesn't mean that you are too late. In chapter ten I talk about how we all need to continue learning throughout all of our lives. These lessons are just as important if you are 30, or 40, or 50 years old as they are if you are young. It is absolutely never too late to make positive changes in your life.

The title of this book implies that these 10 lessons I have identified aren't usually taught in high school. Some of them definitely are. If you were lucky enough to learn some of them in your school, I hope there are a few new insights here that can help you learn or even teach them better. The world is changing every single day, and these lessons will be important, even if the world turns completely around.

The other thing that I included in this book is activities for readers. I included three different types of activities. The first is for students, that is, anyone, of any age, who is reading this book with the intent of making positive personal change. Most of the activities aren't difficult. You just have to choose to do them. If you find a better way to accomplish the same things, you should do that.

The second group of activities is for teachers. That is for anyone who is trying to convey these lessons to others. If you are actually a school teacher you might look at these activities and say "How in the world am I going to fit all of those into my curriculum? We have to prepare for the state assessments and our district wants us to include this, and the Department of Education wants us to include that..." I completely understand what your day looks like; I have been doing it for almost 20 years. That's why I made these exercises very short. You also don't have to do all of them. Maybe some of them fit nicely with your curriculum, maybe some of them don't. Hopefully, some will be useful. Remember that every day you inspire kids to be better. These little exercises are designed to inspire them and give them some useful skills to make their lives better. Mostly, they are designed to help *you* use your personal experiences to show the kids what a positive role model you are.

Finally, I included activities for parents. You are the

foundation on which your child's life is built. It is your values they will see first. It is your values they will be exposed to the most. I once had a conference with the parent of a student who was constantly acting out. The parent was angry because the child wasn't making progress towards better behavior. After talking for awhile, we both realized that the parent's behavior at home wasn't supporting the lessons we were trying to instill at school. Remember, we have the kids for 7 hours a day, and parents have them for the other 17 hours. The kids are going to learn more from you parents than from us, and they trust you more than they trust us, because you are their parents.

One of the themes in my parent activities section is "encourage, encourage, encourage". Being positive and encouraging absolutely does not mean that you have to abandon having rules and strong consequences for breaking those rules. My parents were firm when necessary and encouraging when appropriate, and I am the same way with my son. There is a time for each.

Like I said to the teachers, not all of the activities I propose will work for you. Use the ones that do. Tweak them to make them work better for you. These aren't hard and fast rules, they are only meant to be inspiration.

Some of the things included in this book are easy to do, and others are a little more challenging. They all have one thing in common, you have to make the **CHOICE** to include these lessons in your life. At the end of the day, that's what happiness and success are...a choice.

CHAPTER ONE
YOU HAVE A CHOICE

*"It is our choices... that show what we truly are, far
more than our abilities."*
*- J.K. Rowling, author, in "Harry Potter and the
Chamber of Secrets"*

The idea of personal choice is one of the hardest
concepts for young people to understand. Perhaps it is
because you are just heading out of the dependent stage of
your life and still rely on your parents to make a lot of
choices for you. Whether you like hearing it or not, you are
still dependent on them. I know, that isn't what you want to
hear, but it is a natural part of the process of maturing.

The late Dr. Stephen R. Covey, author of "The Seven
Habits of Highly Effective People", one of the best selling
personal development books of all times, begins his book
by describing the "maturity continuum", because it is so
important.

In Covey's first stage of maturity you are dependent on
your parents and the rest of your older family for the things
you need. In your earliest years, you cannot even get your
own food, clothing, or shelter. You rely on mom and/or
dad for everything.

As you get a little older, you start to develop the skills
you need to be a little more independent each year. Can you
remember the excitement of the first few times you tied
your own shoes? How about the first time someone let you
mow the lawn on your own? These are exciting milestones
in a young person's life. I know it doesn't take long for you
to realize that mowing the lawn isn't really much fun, but
those first few times you do it, you are on top of the world.

Each year the milestones get bigger. When you reach high school, the need for independence grows even more. You want to stay up later or hang out with the friends you choose, or shop for your own clothes that more clearly reflect your personal style. You want to choose your own classes in high school, watch TV shows that you enjoy, or go out with your friends and not have to be home early. These are all clear signs you want more independence, and the freedom to make your own choices.

I once attended a conference of school leaders where there were both elementary and high school teachers. There were sessions specifically for the teachers in each type of school. At the beginning of one of the high school sessions, the college professors hosting us asked what we wanted to discuss. I wanted to know what the kids coming out of high school were lacking when they showed up to college. There were four different things that the professors mentioned. I'll touch on all of them in detail through this book, but the list went like this: writing skills, time management, critical thinking skills, and independence.

In regards to independence, one of the professors went on to tell us several stories about parents who still choose their kid's schedules, parents who call when grades are bad, and parents that choose which organizations their kids belong to.

Don't get me wrong, I hope that every kid, of any age, has a relationship with one or both of their parents in which they are trusted advisors. Parents have been faced with the many of the same decisions kids will be making. We have made a lot of mistakes, and we can save you a lot of pain if you are willing to learn from our mistakes. However, advising and making decisions are two very different things.

When you reach the upper years in high school and definitely in college, you need to make your own decisions, make your own appointments, and address your own problems. You won't be able to take your parents to work with you, so it is important that you learn to function on your own. The way to do this is to make your own decisions. The best way to get your parents to let you make your own decisions is to foster a relationship based on trust.

Why all the talk about choices? It is because your choices will decide whether you live a happy, successful life or one filled with stress and regret. If you do not like the life you are living right now, make the choice to change it. If you want more things out of your life, make the choice to pursue those things. If you want to be happier, make the choice to be a happy person. Each and every one of those things are possible if you make the choice and then have the self-discipline to set and follow the smaller goals that will lead you towards what you want. Leadership, success, and happiness are all choices. You can choose to actively work towards those things, or you can choose to do nothing. One of the most important life lessons that we don't teach you in high school is that *you are in control of your life*. If you don't like how something is going, you can choose to make it better. Like they say at Nike, just do it.

Enemies of Choice

I have my degree in Theater Arts. I also love to read fiction. Studying theater and reading a lot have taught me a few things. The first thing is that I love dramatic conflict. I love man versus man, and man versus nature.

In order for there to be a good conflict we need a good guy and a bad guy, a knight and a dragon, or a very unlucky character and a large animal. In English class you learn that those are the protagonist and the antagonist. Think of the protagonist as a person who has a goal. In this case that's you. The antagonist is anything that stands in the way of that goal. It is the enemy of your goal. It wants you to fail to reach your goal.

Your choices are nothing more than you deciding to reach a goal. You want to have better grades. That is a choice. You want to eat healthier. That is a choice. You want to have more positive friendships. That is a choice. Those are all good things. How can there be enemies of those things? Anything that distracts you from achieving those goals is an enemy, just like the fire breathing dragon is the enemy of the knight in shining armor.

What are the enemies of getting good grades? Television, cell phones, video games, and the internet, especially the very social part of the internet. What are the enemies of eating healthy? Twinkies. I love Twinkies and Ho-Hos and cookies and all of those other delightfully tasty, high calorie snacks. What are the enemies of having a good group of friends? Peer pressure, low self-esteem, lack of confidence, and laziness.

> *"Too many of us are not living our dreams because we are living our fears"*
>
> *–Les Brown, former politician*

Every single thing that you want in your life has enemies and obstacles lining up to stop you from getting there. The very first step in getting what you want is making the choice to go after it.

Here is a list of the most dangerous of the enemies of choice:

Fear: Fear is, by far, one of the biggest killers of choice. It is the king of evil that lives faraway, protected by armies of beasts, big erupting volcanoes, and very large bugs. Fear will stop more good choices from being made than anything else. Even the other enemies of choice that we will look at have fear helping them stop you from making a good choice and succeeding at it.

What do we fear? We fear almost everything. We fear being laughed at. If I had an apple for every kid who doesn't bring up a good idea in a class discussion for fear of being laughed at, I could feed a lot of hungry kids. We fear the unknown. We fear change. We fear rejection. We are programmed from the very beginning of our lives to fear first. It's some kind of survival instinct.

The problem is that fear overreaches. Not only does it keep us from climbing over the fence into the lion's den at the zoo, but it can also keep us from making worthwhile decisions that can change our lives for the better.

Every so often my principal at school will leave me a message that she needs to see me later in the day, but she doesn't tell me what we will talk about. She doesn't do it often, as she is a good leader and knows that leaving people wondering produces fear. But every once in awhile she just leaves me a message to see her after class. From the moment I get the e-mail or voice mail, my mind starts to work. "What did I do wrong?" My inner voice will start to taunt me. I'll run through projects I am working on, or people I have talked to, or things I said in class that might have made someone angry. The majority of the time when I get down there to see her she'll ask me if I want to give my input on which kid to give an award to, or she'll ask if I can help with an upcoming event. It is almost never something bad, and yet that is where my mind usually goes first.

How many opportunities have you passed up because of fear? At certain points in my life, I did not travel to wonderful places because I was afraid that I wouldn't be able to communicate or that the water would make me sick. I have not applied for certain jobs because I was afraid I would get rejected. I have not taken certain risks because I am afraid they won't be successful. I was afraid when I decided to write this book. I asked myself more than once, "What if no one reads it?" or "What if people don't like it?" In the end, I decided I would take the risk. I have fears just like you.

Conquering fear is an ongoing process, and it is really difficult. Just because you can do it one day doesn't mean you can do it every day. What is it that you are most afraid of?

The Inner Voice: Every single one of us has one of these. Sometimes it keeps us up at night. Sometimes it stops us from paying attention to whatever else is going on. Sometimes it drowns out really good advice. A lot of times your inner voice can be mean, or angry, or negative. Often your inner voice takes its cues from fear.

The inner voice's job is to keep you from doing a lot of the good things you could in life. It does this by telling you negative things to make you believe you can't succeed. Sometimes our inner voice says the nastiest things to us, things we would never say to other people.

The most successful people are those who control their inner voice. They have trained their inner voice to be a positive influence on their thoughts. Have you ever seen the cartoons where there is an angel on one of the shoulders whispering positive things into one ear, while there is a devil on the other shoulder whispering negative things in the other ear? The angel and the devil are the two sides of your inner voice. The big question is which one will you choose to listen to? Will you let your inner voice put you down and talk you out of wonderful things, or will you use inner voice to coach you into believing in yourself, so that you can achieve great things?

The people who achieve the most only listen to the positive inner voice and tell the other inner voice to hit the road. Is your inner voice positive or negative.

Lack of Belief: If you really want to make good choices and achieve the great things that come with them, you have to believe that you can, and you have to believe you deserve it.

Not believing that you are capable of something or that you don't deserve something is an express train to failure. Your lack of belief is an enemy to making good choices.

You deserve good things in life. Every person does. If you've made mistakes in the past, that is both alright and common. You absolutely need to forgive yourself first. There is nothing you can do about the past, so don't let it drag you down.

Every single person in this world makes mistakes. It is not the bad decisions that define who you are. It is what you do after those mistakes that defines you. If you continue to make the same bad decisions, it is likely you will feel very negatively about yourself. If you look at your mistakes and see what you can learn from them, then you are turning a negative into a positive.

You absolutely have to see what you can learn from your mistakes, and then you must forgive yourself. This will allow you to truly believe you can achieve your goals, and believe that you actually deserve good things to happen to you. Only then can you really start to feel comfortable making good choices. Do you really, truly believe you deserve good things in your life? Do you believe you can achieve those things if you try?

> *"The thing always happens that you really believe in, and the belief is the thing that makes it happen"*
>
> *– Frank Lloyd Wright, architect*

I have a former student named Adam Page. Adam was born with a condition called Spina Bifida. Without getting too technical, the condition caused nerve damage in his spinal cord which causes Adam's legs not to work like the rest of ours.

As a young boy, Adam's parents believed their son should be able to enjoy sports and an active life like other kids. They made a choice that Adam would not be limited and miss out on all of the things he wanted in life, so they sought out and tried several different sports for Adam to play. Over the years, Adam has participated in karate, horseback riding, baseball and he is still an avid skier. Eventually, Adam discovered sled hockey. It is exactly what it sounds like. All of the players sit on and are strapped into a sled. They use two short hockey sticks like ski poles to propel themselves and to shoot the puck.

Adam started playing sled hockey at the age of six and he really excelled at the sport. He worked hard and believed in himself. In 2007, Adam became the youngest player ever to make the USA National Sled Hockey team, at the age of 15. It was an amazing accomplishment in and of itself.

While playing for the national team, Adam has traveled to places of which he had only dreamed. He has played games in Canada, Germany, and Japan. He has won World Championships and then, in 2010, Adam and his team won the Gold Medal at Vancouver Paralympics. In 2014 he and his team won another gold medal at the Paralympics in Sochi, Russia.

For most people those accomplishments would have been enough. Not for Adam. He has since been asked to speak at many schools and conferences. When I first met him, Adam was very shy and quiet; he seldom said much to anyone. After returning from Vancouver, Adam chose to believe in himself again and was able to conquer his shyness and tell his story in front of 2000 people at a major corporate conference. After he was done there, the CEO of the company hired Adam to speak at several more of their conferences around the country.

Am I done with Adam's story? Not quite. In much of Adam's life, he has to use adaptive equipment, wheel chairs and crutches. When it came time for Adam to learn to drive, a decision had to be made about using an adaptive automobile. Adam believed that he could drive a regular car. After some practice, Adam went out and got his license to drive a car with no adaptations.

Adam's story is one of belief. His parents believed their son should not be limited, and they went and found things for him to do. When they found his passion they supported him to the highest levels of the sport. Adam believed he could do it, and he achieved amazing things. As I am writing this, Adam is only 19 years old, and he has been so many places and done so many things, and it is all fueled by his belief in himself. Adam Page is one of my heroes in life.

If you don't believe you can, your disbelief becomes an enemy of choice. The great Henry Ford said "Whether you think that you can, or think that you can't, you're right." If you don't believe that you can achieve, you are stuck. Your subconscious mind will act in a way that is self-defeating.

Peer Pressure: There are few more powerful forces in our lives than the opinions and the approval of our friends. Most of us have a natural desire to be accepted and appreciated. With this desire being so ingrained in us, it allows for our friends to have a large degree of influence on us.

Peer pressure isn't just for young people. You'll continue to experience it at every phase of your life. Also, it isn't just your friends that exert this kind of pressure; your family can push you in uncomfortable or extraordinary ways, as well.

With so much pressure coming from the people around you, it's difficult to make the choices that you really want. It often seems as though all of your decisions affect other people as well. You want to make choices that make other people happy, sometimes to your own detriment. There are many people who do very destructive things because they are attempting to please other people. I am not just talking about destructive things like drugs, or driving while intoxicated. I know people who have chosen a college major or a job that they hate because they are trying to make someone else happy. Is it worth it to spend all of that money on a college program that you hate? Is it worth it to be in a job that makes you miserable?

While it is important to have people in your life, it is also important to do the things you know are good for you. Those are the good choices. Who are the people that hold the most influence in your life? Are they positive influences or negative ones?

Like belief, peer pressure can go either way. It can influence you positively, or it can influence you in a bad way. Choose positive. Peer pressure got me to write this book. My friends and family kept telling me to do it, so I finally did. I used that influence for the positive. Will you use the influence of others to your advantage, or will you let it sink you?

> *"You can never conquer the mountain. You can only conquer yourself"*
> *- Jim Whittaker, mountaineer*

Lack of Self-discipline: "Everything has a price" is one of the first things I always tell my leadership class. If you want better grades, you will have to create good study habits and put in the extra effort, but it will come at the expense of time with your friends or time on the internet. If you want to make the team, you will have to train and condition harder, and it will come at the expense of watching TV or going to the mall.

In the past few years, I have gained some weight. I don't like it at all, but it is also hard for me to force myself onto the treadmill. More importantly, it is hard for me to not eat cookies, and lots of them. I tell myself that I eat all of those cookies to keep the Girl Scouts in business. My inner voice apparently likes cookies too, and will say whatever is required to get me to eat some. The truth is that I need to discipline myself to eat fewer calories and to exercise more to burn the calories I eat. I am from Buffalo, so I love pizza and chicken wings, and there are a lot of calories in each tasty chicken wing. The second part of my problem is that I don't really love fruits and vegetables that much. Pizza sauce starts out as a vegetable, right? See, now you can hear my inner voice too.

The key is finding the discipline to follow through on your choices. Sadly, sometimes…OK, most times, it is easier to lay on the couch and watch football, hockey, or a good NCIS marathon than it is to go walk a few miles on the treadmill. I absolutely know for a fact that when I exercise regularly, I feel much better, I have more energy, and I sleep better at night. Having the discipline to do it is a whole different story. What are you having problems finding the self-discipline to do?

Tradition: One of the things that is inevitable in life is change. I have worked for my school for almost 20 years, and during that time I have worked for five different principals, and each one came with a new set of ideas. In fact, they were hired because of those ideas. Sometimes the staff bought into the new plans, and other times…well, let's just say it didn't go smoothly. One of the most frequent excuses for not accepting the change? "Well, that's not the way we did it last year." Citing tradition as a reason for inaction is really just another way of saying "I'm too afraid (or too lazy, or too stubborn) to change how we do things".

The only thing holding you back

Do you have friends or classmates who seem to have everything go right for them all the time? They get good grades and make the team or get the lead in the play? As you think about them, are they mostly positive or mostly negative people? Do they seem to fear things? Who do they hang out with? Do they do fun things? Do they give up doing fun things sometimes because they have to do other things?

The most successful people have made choices that have given them the good things in their life. They are willing to pay the price to get those good things and they don't let things like fear, peer pressure, their inner voice, or a lack of belief in themselves get in the way. The most successful and happy people choose to be who they are.

The only thing holding you back is you.

Chapter One Highlights

- Success and happiness are a CHOICE!
- By the time you are in late high school or college, you need to be making your own decisions and handling most of your own affairs.
- There are enemies of choice like fear, peer pressure, a negative inner voice, a lack of self-discipline and tradition.
- The only thing holding you back is YOU!

ACTIVITIES

Students

- Pay attention to what your inner voice is saying. If it is saying something negative, talk back to it. Tell it "no" and replace what it is saying with something positive.
- When you experience some fear or anxiety about something, remember that you are fearing the worst thing that could happen. Stop, close your eyes, and replace that negative image with an image of the best possible outcome. Try to see it in great detail. Focus on it until your fear and tension fades a bit.
- Look at the people in your life. Identify who exerts positive pressure in your life and who exerts

negative. Try to spend more time with the friends that exert positive pressure on you and others.

- Work with your parents to let you make your own decisions. This is a process built on a foundation of trust, so make decisions that earn trust.

Teachers

- Use examples of positive successful people in your content area. Explain their accomplishments. There are successful people in every area.

- Add anecdotes about times you were fearful or connected with bad influences or didn't believe in yourself. Your students will connect with you more. Anecdotes are great ways to make the students feel like they are not in it alone.

Parents

- Coach your kids through their difficult decisions. Point out both positive and negative consequences of their decisions.

- Make your kids make many of their own decisions, and some of their own appointments. They have to learn independence in the late high school years if they are to succeed in college.

- Ask your kids a lot of questions. Let them discover the positives themselves. Discovery is exciting and very satisfying.

- Support them as best you can in the decisions that they make. So long as the decisions don't put your kids or their friends in harm's way, you will have to let them fail; that is how they will learn. Talk to them and help them learn by their mistakes.

CHAPTER TWO
HABITS – THE GREATEST TOOL OF ALL

"We are what we repeatedly do. Excellence then is not an act, but a habit"
- Aristotle, philosopher

Words have connotations. Many words give you a positive or negative feeling as soon as you hear them. It might be argued that the word "habits" has a negative connotation. So often, when they hear the word "habits", people immediately think of biting fingernails, smoking, or poor hygiene. Habits, however, can be good or bad. The best thing about habits is that you can create habits that work to your advantage.

The idea of habits helping with an individual's success is so important that Dr. Stephen R. Covey, who I mentioned earlier, wrote multiple bestselling books on the subject. His, "Seven Habits of Highly Effective People", is the culmination of years of research. His premise is that successful people all displayed a specific group of habits which he describes in detail in his book. It is this group of habits, which work together, that drive people to high degrees of success in their lives.

So, what is a habit? The very first definition listed on Dictionary.com is:

Habit: an acquired behavior pattern regularly followed until it has become almost involuntary: *the habit of looking both ways before crossing the street.*

There are three important parts to this definition. The first significant word in the definition is "acquired". That means you can go out and get it. You aren't born with your habits. Each and every one of them is developed in you and by you.

The second important part of the definition is the words "regularly followed". A habit is something that you do over and over again. Whether it is doing it at the same time each day, or doing it in conjunction with some other activities. It happens frequently and regularly in your life.

The third important part of the definition is the word "involuntary". This means that you do this activity almost without thinking about it. Often these activities become part of a routine, happening in the same order every day. Things like washing your face and brushing your teeth become habits because you do them at the same time each and every day. This firmly implants them in part of your mind that works subconsciously, and you don't even have to think before you do them.

We Are of Two Minds

In your body, the mind is like NASA's Mission Control. Its job is to keep all of the different parts working together smoothly. Think of your mind as having two different parts – the part that works because you tell it to do something and the part that works on its own. For this reason, I liken the mind to a computer.

In a computer you also have two parts. The part of your mind that works on its own is like the operating system. It is like Microsoft's Windows or Apple's iOS. These programs run in the background and have the instructions for all of the things that you never think about. I have absolutely no idea how Windows does what it does. It is the program that lets my finger click on the mouse to tell the computer what I want it to do. It is the program that organizes all of the folders so I can find my files, pictures, or music. It is the program that lets all of the other programs work together. It is already set up when you buy the computer and it does its tasks without us having to tell it what to do.

Your mind has a part that works like this. It does things in the background without an active thought telling it to do them. One of the things that this part of your mind does is to tell you to breathe. You don't stop breathing if you stop thinking about it. You can consciously control your breathing. You can even consciously hold your breath and stop breathing for a short time. Luckily, your mind is smart enough to not let you hold your breath for too long.

The other part of your mind, on the other hand, is the part of your brain that you have to tell to do things. You have to tell it to turn on the TV. You have to tell it to text message your friends. You have to tell it to make popcorn. This conscious part of your mind is like the programs on the computer that do specific things. It is more like Microsoft Word or Adobe Photoshop.

So, how do the two different parts of your mind partner to help you create habits? If there is a part of your mind where things happen without specific commands, how can that help you?

The best part about that part of your mind is that, like the computer's operating system, you can still give it information, and if you do it right, it will begin to follow the instructions. If you are willing to invest the time, you can make it so those things that you want are done in an almost involuntary fashion. You can absolutely commit them to that involuntary part of your mind and create habits.

Creating Habits

Like anything you read in this book, there is a price to pay to achieve it. There are no silver bullets or free rides that will help you to achieve and maintain a successful life. Let me say that again. You have to work to achieve success. Sometimes you get lucky and stumble on to something good, but it will still take work to make sure that long-term success comes out of the good luck opportunity.

The price for creating good habits is that you have to

work at them regularly and consciously in order to commit them to the part of your mind that works subconsciously and make them a habit. You have to brush your teeth every day for awhile until you can stop thinking about it and just do it every night before you go to bed. For the first part of your life, when you are still dependent on your parents, they will act as a reminder to you. Do you remember your parents saying "brush your teeth" every night before you went to bed? As a parent, I remember saying it over and over again, along with things like "look both ways before crossing".

As you get older, it becomes your responsibility to think about the things that you want to turn into your habits. You'll have to write yourself notes or leave yourself other reminder clues to do those things over and over. You won't necessarily think about them regularly until they actually become habits.

The best part about habits? You can form them at any part of your life. You are never too old to create good habits to help you achieve the success you want in life. Whether you are 14 years old or 40, you can create new habits that are very powerful success tools. There's an old saying that you can't teach an old dog new tricks. And yet we hear all the time about people who do amazing things after they retire. My friend, Ed Kilgore, who retired from his job as a sportscaster in Buffalo, climbed Mt. Kilimanjaro at age 63. That took a lot of determination and the creation of some really strong training habits later in life. Go ahead and tell Ed that he's too old to form new habits. I think he'll disagree.

I can see you sitting there saying "Habits..great...sounds easy. How long does it take to form a habit?" I wish there was an easy answer to this. For years the accepted answer was 21-28 days. The problem is that the amount of time it takes to create a habit depends on the self-discipline of the person and the nature of the habit that is being formed.

Here are some examples from my own life. A number of years ago, I was diagnosed with high blood pressure. My doctor gave me a little pill and said "take it once a day". For the first couple of weeks, I left it on the window sill in the kitchen and when I saw it, I would remember to take it. I am not a cook. The only thing I like to make for dinner is a call to the pizza place. So, leaving the pills on the window sill in the kitchen, the room I use the least, was not a good plan for getting me to take it. Needless to say, I didn't form the habit with that plan. I did eventually come up with a much better plan, and very quickly I created the habit that insures I take my medicine and vitamins every day.

I am also trying to live a healthier lifestyle. I have never been an athlete, so exercise has never been a big part of my life. Also, I never really struggled with weight in my life until the past 5 years. My mother is diabetic and I have been getting bigger, so that has been a concern for me. Recently, I have read articles and heard radio reports which touted the health benefits of walking 30 minutes a day. When my grandfather passed away, I ended up with his treadmill in my basement. I am not going to lie, creating the habit of walking 30 minutes a day has been much more difficult than creating the habit of taking my medicine. There is discomfort involved with physical exercise. Sometimes, I am busy and carving out 30 minutes is difficult. Sometimes I don't feel good. I could write a whole separate book on the excuses I tell myself when I am trying to find ways to get out of exercising. It has been a lot harder and taken a lot longer than 28 days to create the walking habit.

So, how long does it take to form a habit? Whether it is 28 days or 100 days doesn't matter. You have to work at it, and you can do anything for a few months, particularly something that will pay such great rewards. In the end, working hard for a few months can pay a lifetime of dividends.

Here are a few different tips that you might find useful to create new habits for yourself.

Using Existing Habits to Create New Ones

Using existing habits is perhaps the most effective way that I can think of to create new ones. Regardless of whether you have ever thought about it before, you have some habits in your life. Some might be good, some might be bad. Your good habits might include setting out your clothes for the next day before you go to bed, or writing a "to do" list every morning before you start your day.

As you become more aware of your existing habits, and are looking for ways to create new habits, you might be able to tie new habits to existing habits. This is how I was able to get into the habit of taking the medication I told you about earlier.

Leaving the medication on the window sill in a room I did not use was a recipe for failure. After a couple weeks of forgetting the medicine, I moved the medicine to the bathroom. I use the bathroom every morning as soon as I wake up to shower and prepare for work, and then again every evening to get ready for bed. At first, I left the medicine on the counter so that I would see it. I decided that morning was best, so now I take my medicine and vitamins with the water I drink after brushing my teeth.

See if there is a habit that you have already established that you can tie your new habit to.

Schedule Your New Habit

Similarly, you can do your new habit at the same time every day, or at least at the same place in your daily routine. What's the difference? I don't get home from work at the same time every day. Some days I have faculty meetings and other days I might have rehearsals for a play that I am directing at school. That means some days I get home at 3pm and others not until 6pm. As soon as I get home from school, I try to jump on the treadmill for my 30 minutes. If I sit down, or start something else, I am not likely to do the exercise.

Reward Yourself

Think about the things that you like to do. Make a deal with yourself that you will tie one of the fun things in your life to your new habit. It's like training a puppy to go to the bathroom outside. If the puppy makes a mess inside he gets yelled at. If a puppy does his business outside he gets a treat. Give yourself a treat for being successful in following through on your new habit activity. Maybe you give yourself a half hour of TV watching, or your favorite snack. It doesn't have to be the same reward every time. Eventually the rewards will pay off as you create the habit and you won't need them anymore Then you can move those rewards to the next habit you are trying to create.

Include Others

Sometimes accountability is the best way to help create a new habit. If you get others involved, they can help by reminding you, or by participating and creating the same new habit for themselves. Yes, misery does love company. This is why there are so many people who go to the gym and work out together. Not only is it a good safety practice to have someone there with you, but it is also a good motivator. It's a good thing when someone is there to push when you are not feeling like doing it, and conversely, you can push your buddy when he or she is less than motivated.

Working together doesn't just apply to physical activity. It could also mean creating a study group with a few of your friends and pushing each other to achieve higher grades. If you meet every Monday after school, this becomes a habit. You can study one subject or many. You can even get together during the summer or other vacations to talk about books you read or current events you see on TV, so that you can stay in the habit of learning. When you get going on making habits, make sure you make expanding your mind one of your habits. This is number seven on Dr. Covey's list of habits that successful people do. He calls it "sharpening the saw". You wouldn't try to cut down a big tree with a dull tool. Your mind is one of your best tools and you need to constantly sharpen it, by reading, learning and exercising it.

Sharing doesn't always mean that someone has to participate with you. They can just be there to congratulate you at your milestones or encourage you when you are feeling down about it. My wife and I are a good team in that respect. When I told her I was sitting down to write a book she didn't say "Oh great, more time away from the family". She said, "I think that's a great idea, you have a lot of good ideas to share." When I say I am going upstairs to write, she leaves me alone and tries to keep the distractions to a minimum. She also asks from time to time how the book is coming along. When the editing process stalled, she pushed me to keep going. Having someone to encourage you is an excellent way to keep moving forward.

"Positive thinking will let you do everything better than negative thinking will."
– Zig Ziglar, author and speaker

Working together is another habit essential to success. The old saying is "the whole is greater than the sum of its parts". In many cases, we work better together, as we draw on the creativity and the insight of others who are around us. Another person's strengths feed our weaknesses and vice versa. Small, focused groups achieve more than the individuals who comprise them. Covey calls this "Synergy" and it is habit number 6 on his list.

Be Positive

This is a habit all by itself. In today's world where there is always someone gossiping about others or pointing out the problems, it is easy to get caught up in the negatives. I'm here to tell you that nothing good ever comes from a negative thought. Think about the most negative person you know. Are they happy and successful? No. They typically have to make themselves feel better by putting other people down.

Being positive is a constant battle. You have to remind yourself over and over not to say bad things about people who say bad things about you or your friends. You have to train your inner voice to say positive things. Because so much of our culture has a tendency to focus on the negative, it takes conscious effort on your part to be positive. You have to be positive about yourself and your abilities, as well as be positive about others.

If you are a positive person, you will achieve much more, and you will become an inspiration to the people around you. People might even look to you to be the person that they include in their goals. That doesn't mean you have to be a work out buddy or study partner for every single person. It means you have to say "How is your workout plan going? You look really great" or "Hey, I heard you got an A in Mr. Herr's class. Great job".

If you have to make one habit for yourself, make it being positive. It's hard, but make it a priority, and you will reap great rewards for you, and for the people around you.

What Habits Should You Create?

Maybe you have specific problems in your life that you would like to address. You want higher grades. You want a promotion at work. You want to feel better. Maybe you just understand that you can always strive to be better at the things that matter to you. Regardless of your goals, there are habits you can form to help you reach them. Sometimes, when do little things regularly, it really adds up to some big results.

Here are some thoughts on habits you can create for yourself.

Better Grades

Study and do homework at a regular time each day. I think the best time for homework is when you get home from school and are still in the academic frame of mind. Find a quiet spot and get your work done efficiently. I don't care what anyone says, you absolutely cannot study better with the TV on, while chatting with friends online, or even with music going on in the background. It splits your brain's processing power and the information you are trying to study doesn't always stick. Homework is practice, designed to commit the material to a spot in your brain. Don't split the processing power. Do your homework in the same spot daily, if possible. You need to be away from distractions. Find a spot that has a nice firm place to write, so that your teachers can actually read your writing or so you can read your notes later. If you do this in a distraction free place, you will spend less time on it and then can get to the fun things more quickly. And remember, the good TV is on later in the evening. After school it's just re-runs.

> *"Reading is to the mind what exercise is to the body." – Richard Steele, Irish writer and politician*

I work at a Catholic school and we have a dress code. Our guys can choose from options, one of which is a dress shirt and tie. I had one student that would not take off his tie when he got home until he had finished his homework. He stayed in school mode right up until he was done with his homework. He felt he performed better if he stayed in the school frame of mind, and his tie symbolized that to him.

Read every day. Maybe you like fiction. Maybe you like biographies of people you admire. Maybe you like military history. Get a book or e-book on your reader and keep it next to your bed. Even reading the sports page or movie reviews helps to expand your mind.

Make it a habit to read for 15 or more minutes every night before you go to bed. First of all, if it is something you like, you will go to sleep with those things that you enjoy in your head. If you study right before you go to bed you will go to sleep thinking about equations you couldn't solve or worrying about the test the next day. Reading something you enjoy helps you to clean out the clutter. Reading regularly also helps you with your writing and communication skills. Reading builds your vocabulary and you learn about good writing by reading good writing. The benefits should be obvious.

Healthier Life

Exercise. You are going to have to do it someday. I was skinny my whole life and thought I would never have to worry about it. I was wrong. It has been a struggle for me every day to stay motivated to exercise because it was not a part of my life for the first 45 years. Work on creating those habits now and they will be easier to keep up with as you get older.

The world renowned Mayo Clinic lists the benefits of regular exercise as weight control, lowering risk of diseases including stroke, heart disease, diabetes and some cancers, as well as improved mood, heightened energy, and better sleep.

People who exercise regularly live healthier lives, feel better, and have more energy. You don't have to run marathons. Just walk for 20-30 minutes a day and you will receive those benefits. Surely you can find a half hour a day. Get up earlier and walk to start your day.

Eat fruits and vegetables. This is another area where I have trouble. I am a carnivore. A meat and potatoes guy. I need to force myself to eat fruits and vegetables. It's easy if you create the habit of eating a piece of fruit with your lunch and vegetables with each meal. This is another habit that will benefit you for all of your life. Rich in vitamins, a regular diet of fruits and vegetables can prevent heart disease, stroke, high blood pressure, prevent some forms of cancer and even protect your eyes from cataracts and macular degeneration. All this according to the Harvard School of Public Health's website.

(http://www.hsph.harvard.edu/nutritionsource/)

Get enough sleep. The truth is, unless you are working a night shift, there really is nothing that you need to do at two o'clock in the morning. That movie will be on again another day, or better yet you can rent it, DVR it, or watch it online. Most people who stay up late chatting with friends online are chatting with people they will see the next day. Train yourself to go to bed at a certain time every day. Teenagers need 8-9 hours of sleep a night and adults need 7-8 hours of sleep a night. If you are not getting enough sleep, your mind is not sharp, and you will be prone to bad moods. In Japan, employers actually encourage workers to take a quick 20 minute nap during the work day. In Spain they have siesta time. They recognize that a quick rest will rejuvenate you better than a cup of coffee or glass of some sugary drink. Sleep is the time where your body rests and repairs itself. There is a reason that we like to sleep when we are sick. Without other stimuli, it is a time that your body can concentrate on itself.

Be organized. Being disorganized is a major contributor to stress. There is nothing worse than not being able to find things you want, or not remembering important events. Think about how much time you currently spend looking for things you need. Try to make a specific place for the really important things in your life. I am a pretty creative guy, so sometimes organization escapes me. I have dedicated, specific locations for the things that I use the most often or are very important to my life. I have a hook that I hang my keys on as soon as I walk in the door. I have a place for my sunglasses. I set up a place where my cell phone and my wallet go every night. I am constantly looking for new organizational methods that will allow me to more quickly find things that I am looking for. These simple things listed above help me with the most important things, and that eliminates some stress from my life. Living in a completely disorganized manner is 100% self-induced stress. Create the habit of putting things in specific locations and it will save you time and stress.

Write things down. Carry a notebook or calendar with you everywhere that you go. Write down important dates, appointments, and assignments all in the same place. Look at your notes often, especially in the morning and at night. First, get into the habit of writing things down. Then, get in the habit of looking at your lists several times during the day. You'll be amazed at your increased productivity.

In the smart phone world we live in, you can write things down in your phone or your tablet. There are apps for calendars, notes, shopping lists, or "to do" lists. You name it. There are many websites like Dropbox.com and Evernote.com where you can store notes or files that are then accessible from any device connected to the internet. It's never been easier to write things down, and keep track of them. You can even schedule reminders for yourself for events or tasks that you need to accomplish.

There are so many things for which you can create habits that will help you to be more successful. The power of creating an automatic action is awesome. Habits are an invaluable tool to achieve the successes that you want. Get started today creating the right habits for the life you want.

Chapter Two Highlights

- A habit is an acquired behavior – you create both your good and bad habits.
- You can put things into the part of your mind that works subconsciously.
- Anyone can create habits.

- It takes about 1-3 months on average to create a habit.
- You can tie new habits to existing habits.
- You can schedule your habits.
- Rewarding yourself is a great way to set habits.
- Including others can help you in forming your new habits.
- Being positive is one of the most important habits you can have.

ACTIVITIES

Student Activities

- Make a list of three things that you want to do or be. Read that list every night before you go to bed and every morning when you wake up.
- Look at your list and choose one thing you could do every day that will help you achieve what you want on your list.
- If you don't already, start keeping a planner that has both your appointments and assignments and a place for you to list your daily tasks.
- Write down a list of 5 rewards you can give yourself when you achieve one of your goals.
- Send at least one positive email, text or social media message per day.
- Make a list of the five most important items in your life and then create a specific place for them when you are not using them.

Teacher Activities

- Include daily planning in your daily routine. It only takes a minute or two to have the kids look at their calendar or their list. It is one of the lessons that my students say was among the most helpful of all that I taught them.

- Send one positive email to a parent each day. I'm a teacher, I know how hard it is to find time in the day. If you can't do it every day, do 5 in one day. They don't have to be long. A few lines of positive thoughts will go a long way.

Parent Activities

- Talk to your kids about your habits. Share with them where you are having your own troubles.
- Help your kids set up good habits by encouraging them to do their homework every day as soon as they get home. Give them quiet time. Encourage them to do it in the same place.
- Encourage, encourage, encourage....but don't nag, nag, nag. (At least not about this) What's the difference? The tone you use and the attitude you bring to it.
- Throw in your own rewards when your kids reach milestones. It doesn't have to be expensive. Go for ice cream, do one of their chores for them. Appreciation goes a long way.
- Send out one positive email, text or social media message per day. It can be to anyone. It gets you focusing on the positive and eventually you will default to looking for positive first, not negative.

CHAPTER THREE
IMAGE IS EVERYTHING

"You never get a second chance to make a first impression"
-Origin unknown

The old saying "Image is Everything" was made popular in the 1990's by an ad campaign for Kodak featuring tennis great, Andre Agassi. As I go through life, I find that idea to be very true. People are hired, or fired, or promoted based on the image they project. Those are three pretty important reasons for you to take conscious control of the things you allow people to see about you.

Being human comes with a lot of benefits. Cable TV, microwave ovens, and hot fudge sundaes are near the top of that list. At the very top, however, is the ability to be self-aware. While it is possible that this ability is not completely unique to human beings, we are certainly in a very small percentage of the inhabitants of planet Earth that possess it.

What self-awareness means is that we are able to focus our attention on ourselves and through that focus, we are able to see our own knowledge, our own attitudes and our own opinions. We are able to look at our behavior and compare it against a set of inner standards or values. We can actually think about ourselves and see where we stand against other members of society. That is to say, we can step outside ourselves and see our lives as if we are an outside observer.

The best part about being human and being self-aware is that we have the capability to look at ourselves, see things we don't like, and change them. While certain animals may possess degrees of self-awareness, they have little capacity for change. Humans, on the other hand, absolutely can change if we don't like our situation. As I said at the beginning of this book…Leadership, success and happiness are a choice. Being self-aware allows us to see when we are unhappy with our self or our life and then change it.

Your Image and Brand

Every person has an image. You are the quiet kid, the smart girl, the athlete, the caring guy, the hard working lady, or the jerk. Your image is completely up to you. In business they call your image your "brand", and businesses spend millions of dollars to define, design and protect their brand. They absolutely want to control exactly what it is that their customers see about them.

What makes up your image or brand? Every single thing that people can see about you. Every single thing that allows them to make a decision about who they think you are. Every single thing: how you talk and what you say, how you dress, how you treat other people, how hard you work, or don't work, how helpful you are to others, how well you keep your promises, how punctual you are, how polite, and respectful you are. Every single thing.

In the old days, when I was in high school, we had almost complete control over our own image. Maybe our names got mentioned in a note passed from one girl to another, but that was it. It was a very limited audience outside of our own small group. Nowadays, however, it is much more challenging to keep complete control of our image.

In his book, "Digital Leader", author Erik Qualman discusses our life in the digital era. He asserts that each of us has a digital stamp that follows us throughout our whole life and eventually becomes our legacy. Our digital stamp is made up of *digital footprints*, things that we post about ourselves online, and *digital shadows*, things that other people post about us online. This digital stamp is a huge part of our overall image now. One of the first things a potential employer does is to Google a job candidate to see if their digital stamp tells them anything negative about the candidate. Like it or not, an internet search is part of your resume now. People do not get hired, or even lose their jobs over their digital stamp.

How Do People See You?

Take a moment to think about how people perceive you. When your name comes up in conversation, what do people say? Do they see you as someone they can turn to when they are in need, or do they see you as someone who is too stuck on themselves to be of help? Do they see you as someone who is knowledgeable and willing to share that knowledge, or do they see you as someone who is so competitive that you will keep that knowledge to yourself to give yourself a competitive advantage? Do they see you as compassionate, or as cold and uncaring? How do other people perceive you?

How Do You Want People To See You?

Ultimately, the more important question is how you want people to see you? Once you make the decision about what you want people to think of you, you can choose (yes, there's that word again) to act in a way that supports that image. While you can't always control people's perception of you, you can feed that perception with positive actions that will support the image you want.

Do you want to be known as someone who is helpful? Be assertive and ask people if there is anything you can do to help. However, keep in mind, if you ask, and then don't deliver, you will create exactly the opposite image that you were hoping for. If you ask and then don't follow through, then you become insincere.

If you want to be known as someone who is a hard worker, then work hard. Limit your distractions and put your effort into getting the job done, whatever it is. If you want to be known as a good leader, then lead by example. Don't ask people to do jobs that you wouldn't do yourself.

In addition to being a teacher, I was in charge of our school's Buildings and Grounds Department for many years. When things were busy, I pitched right in and helped sweep the floors or shovel the snow. It wasn't really my job, but it showed my employees that I was not just there to boss them around. I was there to get the job done and I was willing to roll up my sleeves and pitch in.

The lesson here is that you get to decide what you want people to think about you and then you can do very specific things to support that image. This might be the easiest thing you can learn from this book.

When people talk about the idea of perception versus reality, the conversation usually ends with the statement that perception is not reality. I disagree. If someone has a bad perception of you, that is very definitely their reality. And nowadays, if someone has a bad perception of you, it can spread quickly because of easy access to the internet and social media. Did this ever happen to you? You have a fight with someone and suddenly it turns up as a post on someone's social media page? A disagreement between two people gets shared with 100, or 200, or 300 people. Because of the reach of these social networks, a small disagreement can easily turn into a much bigger deal with the click of a mouse.

First Impressions

First impressions are powerful things. People make decisions about others very quickly, and change them slowly, if at all. We can make first impressions from across the room, or down the hall. We make first impressions when we are not even present, through information or pictures we post on the internet. Sometimes we don't even post the information. It could be anyone with a camera that captures images or video of us and posts it. Each of these things contributes to other people's immediate and often permanent decision about who we are. Think about how quickly you form opinions about people you meet.

Who Controls Your Image?

Here we go again with that word "choice". You're going to hear it over and over again. Who controls your image? You do, through the choices you make. It begins with some thinking about what you want people to see when they look at you. After that, you make a choice about the actions you can do to support the image you have created in your mind. You see your image in your mind first, and then you take steps to create it in reality.

Sometimes, this just doesn't work and no matter how hard you try, people can be mean. Maybe they are jealous, or maybe they have low self-esteem and can only lift themselves up by bringing other people down. This happens everywhere there are groups of people. It happens in schools. It happens at work. It happens in church groups and on sports teams.

You can't control what other people do or think, even in regards to you. What you can control is your reaction to what they do. If your reaction is heated, that says something about you. If your reaction is gracious, that also says something about you. When my son used to come home from middle school he would sometimes be angry and say things like "I hate it there. Kids are saying that I am _____(fill in the blank)" I would say to him "Don't worry about it. If you react, then it is fun for them. If you don't react, they will usually stop because it is no fun". So, while you can't control what people do, your reaction says volumes about who you are. Take a minute to think about your reaction, and measure it against the image that you want people to see. Ask yourself, "Does this action help or hurt the image I am trying to portray?" Strive to act only in ways that help you create and support the image you want.

Building Your Image

What things can you do that will help you to improve the way others perceive you? Here are some simple image building tips.

Put yourself together – The very first impression people get of you is often when they see you for the first time. Make sure you are put together. This doesn't mean you have to run out and buy the most expensive clothes. Nor does it mean you have to be dressed up everywhere you go. It means you have to work with what you've got. Comb your hair, keep yourself clean, brush your teeth, wear your clothes the right way. Clothing is a great way to express yourself, however it is also important to wear clothes that are appropriate for the place you are. It's OK to be comfortable and wear sweat pants around the house, but not to a job interview or a funeral. Sometimes you can have your shirt untucked, sometimes it should be tucked in. A nice shirt that is tucked in correctly looks great, whether it cost $9 or $29. I like to dress nicely and I frequently buy inexpensive things or sale items. You can never go wrong with modesty.

Think before you talk – Take a minute to choose your words. Will whatever you are about to say add value to the conversation or will it be destructive to the project or to another person? My mom used to say all the time "If you haven't got anything nice to say, don't say anything at all". That is some of the best advice I have ever gotten in my life. If you aren't going to add value, keep your mouth shut. Nothing positive ever comes out of negative words. People judge you on what you say.

Show respect – This is a big one. I am always inspired and impressed by people who have served in our military. Obviously, the sacrifice and selflessness that they display by choosing to serve their country is awesome. Another thing that I notice frequently in people who have a military background is that they start from a position of respect. There's this misconception that respect has to be earned. I don't believe that is true. I show respect to plenty of people that I don't know, or don't even necessarily like. Everyone deserves common courtesy, and that is a form of respect. Extending courtesy and kindness, even to people you don't like, gives them space to earn your respect, and shows that you are a good person.

Service men and women ooze respect in their words. They address people that they just met as "sir" and "ma'am". This is a simple thing that says a lot about you, particularly if you are a young person. When you offer someone a firm handshake, look them in the eye, and say "Pleased to meet you, sir (or ma'am)," 9 times out of 10, you've got their attention.

Exercise humility – Great leaders are not possible without great supporters. If you think it is your skills and your skills alone that bring you to success, you are incorrect. Your success in school is in part due to your teachers, your family, your friends, and your teammates. Your success at work is partly due to your co-workers, and your supervisors. Don't get me wrong, there are bad teachers and bad bosses in the world, but quality people always find a way to learn or to be productive in a bad environment. My point is that there are always people supporting you and when you are successful, remember to thank them for their help.

I am the club advisor for the Tech Crew at my school, which runs the stage lights and sound for all of our events. Every so often, they don't get a verbal "thank you" at the end of the event when thanks are being offered. Early in the year, new members will sometimes catch this and mention it. I've always tried to teach them that we don't do this job because we get thanked at the end or get our name in the program. We do the job because it needs to be done.

Keep Your Promises – I have worked with a lot of people in my career. My favorite people are the people who teach me things along the way. One of my good friends, Ed Hokaj, is a retired guy who has volunteered at our school. Many of Ed's own kids attended our school and his son met his wife there. Recently, Ed's grandchildren have been students there. Ed used to work at IBM and he and I became friends when he volunteered to be on our school's Board of Directors. I was the Technology Coordinator at the time and with his computer experience he chaired the Technology Committee.

We had a pretty big task in front of us. There wasn't a lot of technology in the school at the time, so we were building from scratch. When we first met, I was a bit overwhelmed. He would ask me to do things or I would volunteer, but then I would not always get things done, and that created a very negative image of who I was. One day, he finally sat me down and in his no nonsense way he said, "Listen, if you aren't going to do it, don't say it." I carry that advice around with me every day. Telling people you are going to do things and then disappointing them is a great way to leave people with an unfavorable opinion of you.

Volunteer – There is no better feeling than helping out someone in need. Most times it only takes a few minutes, which may be a very small sacrifice for us, but means the world to someone else. Additionally, it sets you apart from others as a go-to person, and the go-to person is always the most valuable person in the room. The great leadership teacher, Dr. John C. Maxwell even has a book that is titled "Talent Is Never Enough". Talent isn't enough. You have to work hard too. Be a go-to person.

Your online image is still your image – There are a few important things you should think about as you are posting things online. First and foremost, there aren't different versions of you for different circumstances. What you willingly post on a social media website is absolutely a reflection of who you are. When you write nasty things about people or bully them, people see that. On the other hand, when you write nice or inspirational things, people see that as well.

My friend, Larry Roth, is a partner in a large company that specializes in corporate branding. He is responsible for developing brands using the internet and social media. In a recent conversation we had, Larry said, "I think the real opportunity for new graduates is to have a strong internet presence, with positive community reputation points. It's not enough to not be in a negative light on the internet. You have to have positive things, as well." This guy is a professional at using the internet to brand companies and he is telling kids that they need actively work to build positive images on the internet if they want to be considered for good jobs.

Many employers are now looking at a person's social media before they hire them. In some cases, your social media persona is a better predictor of who you really are than your resume or your interview. More and more companies are actually firing employees because of their behavior on a social media site. And, as the competition to get into good colleges intensifies, more college admissions people are admitting that they look at social media sites in order to choose between candidates. Party pictures really don't prove to anyone that you are a good choice as a student or an employee.

Nowadays, social media websites are filled with angry posts. People insulting each other and screaming down others who disagree with them. I am not proud to say that I've even caught myself participating in that. It's OK to have strong opinions, but it's important to realize that other people are entitled to their beliefs as well. Getting angry and insulting because people disagree with you is not acceptable. It shows your inability to listen to, respect, or get along with other people and that is a very unattractive quality in you. Why would anyone want to hire a person like that?

I cannot emphasize enough the importance of the image that you present. People have a perception of you and what that perception is can either help you or hurt you greatly. The best news is, you can control most of that perception through your choices. In fact, you can carefully and thoughtfully craft the image that you want people to see.

Chapter Three Highlights

- Because we are self-aware, we can see ourselves and we can decide when we don't like our circumstances and then choose to change them.
- We all have an image or brand.
- We can decide what we want our image to be and then develop an action plan to show that image to others.
- We control our own image.

ACTIVITIES

Student Activities

- Write down three things you would want people to say about you after you moved away from the area you live in now.
- Write down two specific things for each of those that you could do regularly to make sure that is how you are remembered.
- When you meet someone older than you, look them in the eye, offer them a firm but not overpowering handshake, and call them "sir" or "ma'am".
- Never, ever let poor manners creep into your life.
- Dress appropriately for the event you are attending. How you dress reflects how important you feel an event is.

Teacher Activities

- Add famous people who have a positive image to your lesson plans. Those people are already there. They are people like Abraham Lincoln, Thomas Edison, Susan B. Anthony, and Jane Goodall. Every content area has people who have a positive image. Point them out. Those are the role models for our kids.

- Never, ever allow student poor manners to creep into your classroom. (Easier said than done, I know.)

Parent Activities

- Expect your kids to put themselves together for certain events. There is no excuse to dress sloppily for weddings, funerals, graduations, job interviews, school concerts, and award ceremonies. You have to lead by example here.
- Never, ever accept poor manners or a lack of respect. This is not negotiable. Bringing your child up to be a well-mannered person is one of the most important things you can do for them. The best way to do this is to lead by example. Pay attention to how you speak when referring to or addressing others.

CHAPTER FOUR
VALUES ARE THE
FOUNDATION

"When your values are clear to you, making decisions becomes easier."
- Roy Disney, former executive Walt Disney Company

What is it that you value the most? Is money most important to you? Is family most important to you? Is being famous most important to you? We will absolutely act in different ways, depending on what we find to be the most important thing, or the "center" in our lives. We focus on the things that are at our center, and when we focus on things we tend to act in a way that helps us get to those things.

Finding Your Center

Take a look at some of the people you know. Is it possible for you to see, by their actions, what is the most important thing to them? If you stop to look, it is often pretty apparent. The person who never wants to go out, or complains about the price of things may be the money-centered person. The person who is always going to their brother's or sister's games or concerts, or bragging about their sibling's many accomplishments is the family-centered person. The person who is always trying to be in the spotlight will probably spend their life seeking fame.

Can you have more than one center? Absolutely. Many people have more than one thing that is very important to them. Once again, you are in control. You have a choice. Don't let your center just set itself. Decide what you want to be important to you and then focus on it daily. That will become your center.

43

Where Do Our Centers Come From ?

There are three words that often get confused with each other. They are all similar, but they are definitely not the same thing. These three things are **MORALS, VALUES,** and **ETHICS.**

Morals

Morals are the compass by which we see right and wrong. We judge ourselves and we judge others by this compass. Morals are set not only by ourselves, but by the society and culture in which we live. In some cultures it is OK to do things that we would absolutely find wrong in our society. For example, in some countries, women are treated more like property than people. I'm glad that is morally unacceptable where I live.

Morals guide our behavior. We agree that it is bad to lie or to steal things. We know that it is good to be kind or help the poor. There are behaviors that are definitely linked to our morals and people who behave in a way that is in contrast to them are labeled as immoral people by society.

Values

Values are the things that we hold important in our lives. We give them worth in our lives. Values are something we determine individually, whereas morals are driven by society.

Our values, like our morals, also influence our behavior, but in a slightly different way. In a moral sense, we know that lying is wrong. The value that would correspond to that is honesty. We talked earlier about people who value money. It is not immoral to value money, unless you end up stealing or cheating people to get the money. There are very honest people out there that value money and are willing to work very hard and in an honest way to make their money.

Values can be almost anything. One of the things that I value most is creativity. I don't like to get involved with projects where I cannot use my creativity. Here's a small list of other values. It is not complete, by any means.

Humility	Tolerance
Courage	Influence
Equality	Celebrity
Forgiveness	Power
Hard Work	Religion/Faith
Kindness	Learning
Charity	Fun
Compromise	Integrity
Generosity	Gratitude
Honesty	Respect
Trust	Responsibility
Patience	Family
Purity	Money

Each and every place you look for a list of values, you will find a different list. That's OK. Values are personal and reflect the things that you hold dear in life. We each have different words to describe what we hold dear and it's good to define it for yourself.

While we don't need to get too hung up on what we call things, we should take the time to identify the things that we hold most important in our lives. Having a clear picture of what is important allows us to focus our activities in areas that fulfill our inner needs. Maybe you haven't realized it yet, but if you never feel better than after you work with underprivileged kids, or after you volunteer at a soup kitchen, it might indicate that service and/or charity are central values to you. Once you know this, you can plan more activities that fulfill that. Once you recognize it, maybe you will even make a career out of your value by working at a not-for-profit organization that helps people who need it.

Where Do Values Come From?

Are you born with your values? Absolutely not. There is no chromosome that decides what is important to you. Your values are a work in progress from the day you start to comprehend things until the day you die. They change because of people you know. They might change because you make a choice to make something important in your life, or because of events in your life.

In March of 1994 my daughter Rebecca was diagnosed with a rare, cancerous brain tumor. In November of 1995, she passed away at only 5 years old. I learned so much in that 21 months, and in the years that immediately followed. Those years were filled with anger, grief, alcohol abuse, a teetering marriage and a whole lot of personal discovery. The experience completely changed my values. After the dust settled and I figured things out, I think I became a better dad, husband, and even a better teacher. I made major changes in my values after my daughter died from cancer. It affected me in positive ways that I could never have imagined. That's what we mean when we talk about "life-changing events".

Your values are formed from all sorts of stimuli. Your parents and immediate family are the primary source. Eventually, your friends, the media, and the outside world start to do their part to help shape your values.

Let's not forget your experiences. The events in your life and the environment in which you are brought up absolutely help to shape your values. A kid who was brought up in a poor family may place a much higher value on a small act, gift or opportunity than a child who was brought up having everything that they wanted in life. A child that was brought up in a rough neighborhood, living in fear will certainly value safety and trusting relationships more than kids who never had to fear anything.

Values are complex, and are formed by many different factors. Each of us has a different set, and they can change throughout our lives.

Ethics

Another word that gets tossed around with morals and values is ethics. Ethics are more like morals, in that are agreed upon by a group. Ethics often refer to the behavior of someone in a professional setting. It is not ethical for a doctor to disclose information about a patient. It is not ethical for a lawmaker to take money or gifts from someone who is applying for a job or contract with the government.

Our morals and values will drive whether we behave in an ethical fashion.

Living Your Principles

A good discussion of morals, values and ethics is important because it will help us to create a happy life. The road to happiness is definitely paved with our values. If we value it, that means we want it. If we have what we want, that definitely makes us happy. So, once we identify what it is we value the most, we can work towards fulfilling those needs. If you live according to your principles, you will certainly be happier, particularly if those principles are in harmony with the morals that drive your particular culture.

A word of caution: earlier I said that you can value money. That is true. Having money, however, does not insure happiness. If you value money solely as a possession and just spend your life accumulating it, that won't necessarily make you happy. Money is a tool. If you use it to accomplish other things, then it can make you happy.

Having a bank account full of money will not generally make you happy in and of itself. Having money can represent other things, like freedom. You can travel. Money can relieve some of the stress when things go wrong, which they inevitably do. You can use it to help others, if you choose. So, it is what you can do with the money that is appealing, not just having it.

Each of us has our own set of values and principles. If those principles are in harmony with the morals of our society, and if we live in a way that is consistent with our values, we can live a very happy life.

What are the things that you value most in your life?

Roles

The final step in defining ourselves and managing our image is to identify the roles that we play in the world. We are different things to different people, and identifying those roles is important because it allows us to prioritize them.

I am no longer a kid, and the primary roles that I play are: father, husband, son, brother, teacher, director, mentor, and friend. There are others like employee, and back when I was younger and still played sports I was a teammate. I'm an American. I'm an author. I bet with enough time I could come up with 50 or 75 roles I play to different people. I said that the roles above were my primary roles. These are the ones that I have identified as the most important to me. These are the ones that I spend time making sure I am the best that I can be at them.

As I wrote them, I put them in the order of importance to me. Take a look and see if you can identify what is most important to me in life from that list. First is my family and after that are my roles as someone who helps others to learn and grow. Those are the things that I am most passionate about. Those are the things that make me get up in the morning. Notice that wage earner isn't on that list. I figure if I work hard on those things, the money will come, and it has. My whole life I have been able to focus on those roles and I have worked my way up to near the top of almost every organization where I have been employed.

What are the roles that you play in life? What order of importance would you put them in?

Now that we have taken some time to get to know ourselves in this chapter, we can move forward and make choices that will move us towards success.

The Mission Statement

One of the tools that a business uses to keep on track is the mission statement. Some businesses spend large sums of money to develop their mission statement. They hire expensive consultants to come in and guide their company through a meticulous process of developing a concise mission statement that will be the guiding principle in business operations. Mission statements are for businesses of all sizes. It is very helpful to have a clear guidepost against which you can measure each and every decision.

Here's some examples of some mission statements from the websites of companies that you might recognize.

Nike – "To bring inspiration and innovation to every athlete* in the world."

Facebook – "Facebook's mission is to give people the power to share and make the world more open and connected."

Starbucks – "to inspire and nurture the human spirit – one person, one cup and one neighborhood at a time."

Pepsi – "Our mission is to be the world's premier consumer products company focused on convenient foods and beverages. We seek to produce financial rewards to investors as we provide opportunities for growth and enrichment to our employees, our business partners and the communities in which we operate. And in everything we do, we strive for honesty, fairness and integrity."

Some mission statements are very short, while others are longer and address more issues. In any case, if your mission statement doesn't reflect who you are and what you want to achieve, it will not be useful. By committing the mission to writing, it gives the managers and employees a reference point against which to see if the decisions that the company is making daily are in line with the company philosophy.

Starbucks talks about inspiring and nurturing the human spirit. If they were to buy coffee from countries that used slave labor to grow and harvest the beans, that would not be very inspiring or nurturing. In accordance with their mission, Starbucks will only buy coffee from vendors who provide high-quality coffee and provide it using business practices of which they approve. In the book "The Starbuck's Experience: 5 Principles for Turning Ordinary into Extraordinary", author Joseph Michelli talks about Starbuck's principle of being considerate.

"For Starbucks, at the corporate level, "being considerate" means exploring the long-term well-being of partners and those individuals whose lives the partners touch, all the while being mindful of the earth's ability to sustain the demands that Starbucks places on it."

The coffee is more expensive, but in order to stay true to their mission, Starbucks is willing to pay more, and so are their customers.

The great thing about a mission statement is that it isn't only useful for a business. You can write your own personal mission statement, and create that measuring stick by which to hold yourself accountable.

Is It Hard To Write A Personal Mission Statement?

It isn't difficult to write your own personal mission statements, because there are no rules. Your personal mission statement is, by definition, personal. It is only for you to be able to look at as you make decisions in your life. You can take the simple approach like Starbucks or Nike and make it one sentence, or you can go the route of Pepsi and write something longer and more specific.

To start your personal mission statement, take a look at the list of values that you created earlier. Write down the values that you identified as most important. Now look at the roles you play. Decide which are the most important of those roles? Once you have identified the values and roles that are most important to you, you can create a mission statement that stays true to those. It does not have to address each and every one of them individually, but it cannot conflict with any of your values either.

Be creative. If you want to write a poem, write a poem. If you want to use bullet points, use bullet points. This is only for you, and you should write it in a way that makes you happy.

Here's three examples of personal mission statements:

- *I will live each day with a sense of humility, a sense of service, and a sense of humor. These three things will help bring smiles to the world.*

- *Learning and teaching walk hand in hand, so each and every day I will strive for both.*

- *Music is a way to say out loud the things that many people only think. My music will bring voice to the wonderful things that reside quietly in other people's souls.*

Once you have created your first draft of your mission

statement, walk away from it for awhile. Let it sit and simmer. After a few days or a week, come back and see if it still rings true to you. If it doesn't, make some changes. If it does, commit to it by writing it or printing it someplace where you can look to it for inspiration. Sometimes when I am having a bad day, looking at my personal mission statement can remind me of what I am about. Sometimes when I have a very difficult decision to make, I put my personal mission statement in front of me and I measure each of the possibilities against my mission. It centers my thoughts and allows me to see what course of action will best allow me to be true to myself. All in all, it only took me a few hours to write my mission statement, but when it comes to making decisions, having it with me to measure my choices by has saved me more time than that. It also helps me make decisions that are in alignment with my beliefs.

Some people would probably think it is not cool to write a personal mission statement, but the best part is that you write it in private and keep it somewhere private, so no one even knows you wrote it unless you tell them. There's a reason it is called a "personal" mission statement. What's holding you back from creating this invaluable tool for yourself? Find a quiet place and get started.

Chapter Four Highlights

- We all have a center in our life and identifying it will help us to live a life fulfilling our needs.
- Morals are usually accepted by societies and cultures and help us decide what is right and wrong.
- Values are more individual and reflect what we hold most dear in our lives.
- Ethics are rules set by groups that we belong to.
- It is very important to define our values and live according to them.
- We all play a variety of roles in our lives and it is essential to know which ones are most important to us.

- Businesses use mission statements to keep them moving towards their ultimate goals.
- People can use personal mission statements to clearly define who they are and what is important to them. Personal mission statements are an excellent tool to help make important decisions.

ACTIVITIES

Student Activities

- Make a list of the three most important things to you. Use the list of values listed in this chapter to help you out.
- Make a list of activities that you could do regularly that would support those values you have identified.

Teacher Activities

- As you talk about famous people in your content area, have students identify what they think those people's values are/were. Then point out what you think that person's values are. Again, these famous and successful people are role models to our students.

Parent Activities

- Discuss the importance of values with your kids. Tell them what yours are, but remember that your actions will speak louder than words. If you say that family is the most important thing, but always find excuses not to go to family events, the kids will see that contradiction. If you claim honesty is important to you and then lie about your kid's age to save a dollar off the ticket price at the zoo, your children will pick up on that as well.
- Remember not to force your values on your kids. They will learn from seeing you in action. If you want to hold charity as a value, then give together. If

you want them to hold service as a value then volunteer together.

CHAPTER FIVE
GOALS ARE THE ROADMAP TO SUCCESS

"A goal properly set is halfway reached"
- Zig Ziglar, author and motivational speaker

Back in the days before GPS apps on our phones or on our dashboards, when planning a trip we had to look at a map. We had to know where we wanted to go and we had to use a map to figure out the quickest, or the safest, or the most scenic way to get there, depending on our priorities.

Life is kind of the same thing. We need to decide on a place that we would like to be, and then we need to set up a route to get there. The "place we want to be" doesn't necessarily have to be a geographic location. One of the "places" I want to be is to become a published author. If you are reading this, my map worked. It was definitely a map that got me here. I decided on a destination and I set up a series of steps to get me to my goal. Once I achieved each of the small steps, in order, I found myself sitting in my office staring at a finished manuscript. That journey was complete.

An ancient Chinese philosopher named Lao Tzu said "The journey of a thousand miles begins with a single step". It's fitting in two ways. First, you have to choose to take a journey. In our case, we have to choose what it is we want to achieve. Secondly, we have to take action. It's easy to sit around and hope that the things you want appear on your doorstep, but unfortunately, that doesn't happen often. You have to choose to actively pursue the things that you want in life. They will not come to you. The key is knowing what you want and designing an action plan to get there.

One of the most important things you need to know at this point is that everything has a price. I don't necessarily mean dollars and cents, but there is always something you will have to pay to get what you want. If you want to lose weight, you will have to pay the price of less junk food and more exercise. If you want to have money in the bank, you will have to save more money or buy less stuff. (It is, after all, just stuff.) As you are looking at things that you want to achieve, just remember, you will have to pay a price to get it.

Goals

When we start talking about making real goals, we aren't talking about little things. Little things will happen on their own. Goals need to be larger. After the last chapter, you should have more of a feel for what your values and roles are. It is important that the things you want in life don't conflict with those. If they do, either you have to shift your values or you have to change your goals. If your goals are in conflict with your values, you'll never reach them.

Big goals, which are what we are talking about here, have a tendency to just materialize in our minds. As we study courses in high school or college, maybe a career path develops. As we work our job, maybe a plan materializes to travel to some exotic location. As we look at ourselves in the mirror over months, maybe the desire grows to look and feel better. These type of goals are cultivated over time in the part of our mind that works subconsciously before they make the jump to our conscious mind.

Here's a great example. Over the past year or so, I have been more and more impressed with people who travel. When I was younger, my family traveled the United States fairly extensively. We took a cross country trip and we had been up and down the East Coast as well. Other than a few border towns in Mexico or a fishing camp in Canada, I hadn't done any international travel.

Since getting married, my traveling became much more predictable. We did the Disney trips and enjoy a family trip pretty regularly to Hilton Head Island, South Carolina.

What we didn't do is go anyplace exotic, like tropical islands or European vacations.

As I watched the occasional travel show, I became more intrigued by these exotic locations. Finally, my wife and I decided that we wanted to take a really cool vacation with our son to celebrate his graduation from high school. Since I knew that my son's life was about to get busy with internships and jobs, and this might be our last family vacation for quite awhile, I wanted it to be cool.

We sat down and laid out plans. After narrowing it down, our three choices were a cross country flight and a drive up the West Coast, a trip to Europe, or a Caribbean cruise. We have traveled the US, so we dumped the cross country thing. Europe was too expensive on the short schedule we had to save up the money. So the cruise was the winner. We wanted the most exotic thing we could do in our price range, so we picked a cruise that left out of New Orleans and visited two ports in Mexico, one in Honduras, and one in Belize.

> *"If you want to reach a goal, you must "see the reaching" in your own mind before you actually arrive at the goal."*
>
> *– Zig Ziglar, author and motivational speaker*

It was absolutely an amazing trip, and the idea came from seeing exotic places on TV. It is amazing how your mind works. The key is seeding it with good, positive thoughts and goals.

Visualizing

The first step in setting goals is to visualize your end

result. This is a two step process, and it is a very powerful tool. Many of the world's best athletes visualize making the shot or hitting the ball right before they actually do it. Whether they use visualization in practice or pre-game, or even during the game, they do it because it works for them. Seeing their goal in their mind first helps them achieve their goal.

So, the first step of the process is to actually see, in your mind, the end result that you want to achieve. Whether it is making the putt or graduating from college, it is important to see it very clearly in your mind. Some people can see things in their mind at any place and time. Others need a quiet place to be able to visualize. Find whatever place is best for you and begin to visualize the end results that you want, right away.

The second step in the process is to then insert yourself into the picture. **See yourself enjoying the end result that you want.** Maybe it is seeing yourself standing in front of an applauding audience after you made a great speech, or maybe it is seeing yourself being congratulated after you land the big promotion. If you can firmly set in your mind the image of you enjoying your accomplishment, it will begin your subconscious mind working on achieving this goal. Get the image in there and then revisit it often. It can help to create a short phrase that you can repeat to yourself as you revisit the image.

Once you have the image, try and revisit it every night as the last thing you do right before you go to sleep. Sometimes happy images before bedtime help us to sleep through the night. Also, our subconscious mind does some of its best work while we are sleeping. Then its negative cousin, your inner voice, can't get in the way.

Dr. Stephen Covey, in "The Seven Habits of Highly Effective People" calls this first step the "mental creation". He maintains that you have to create something in your mind first, and then you can go out and create it in reality.

Goals

Once you have that first mental creation, the destination, you can go about setting the smaller goals you need to get there. If I were driving from my home in Buffalo to Florida, I would have to break the trip up into two or three steps to get there. When I was younger I might try to drive the full 21 hour drive in one shot, but I have gotten older and smarter. I realized it was not a good or safe way to make the trip.

I might break it up in a couple of different ways. I might break it into two 10-11 hour driving days. I'd use the Internet to help me figure out where the logical stopping point is and then book my hotel and drive there. A second solution would be to pick some nice spots I wanted to see and break it up into three 7-8 hour days. Now I would have three specific stopping points or goals and I can measure my success each day.

SMART Goals

I like to hope that all of my goals are smart, but certainly that isn't always true. That's why I determine whether they are by using SMART as an acronym. It stands for the words specific, measureable, attainable, relevant, and timely. If you frame your goals using these guidelines, you'll have a much better chance of achieving them.

Specific

There is no better way to make sure you fail than to have fuzzy goals. Goals like "I want to be happy" aren't easily achievable. We all have different definitions of happy, and there are actually multiple things in every one of our lives that will make us happy. Pizza makes me happy. Travel makes me happy. Reading makes me happy. Lots of things can make you happy. Think of what it is that makes you happy and is something that you want to achieve, and make that your specific goal.

Another one of my favorites is "I want to have a good paying job". Guess what? I do too. There are tons of good paying jobs out there. I can't do them all. Actually, I can't do most of them. You wouldn't want me removing your spleen or cooking your fancy dinner. Those aren't my skills. As you start looking for a career, you need to be specific about what it is you are looking for. Even if it is just specific with yourself, for the time being. It helps you focus on finding that job. So, making the statement more specific might be something like this. "I want a good paying job in the education field". The more specific, the better.

Measurable

Another good way to fail is to not have milestones that you can reach. In my drive to Florida example, I know the total drive from my house to the Tampa area is about 21 hours. That knowledge allowed me to divide the trip into 2 or 3 specific length drives. I knew exactly what I had to do to achieve my overall goal of driving 21 hours.

Here's some other examples. Losing weight would make me happy. Saying I want to lose weight is specific, but not measurable. Saying I want to lose 20 pounds is specific and measurable.

Another great goal is saving some money. You are never too young or too old to start this. Saying I want to save money is OK. Really looking at your budget and saying I want to put $25 per week away is a much better approach. You may have to give up one order of pizza and wings a week, but you know exactly how much that you have to sacrifice. The best part is that at the end of the week you have 25 extra bucks. At the end of the month you have an extra $100 and at the end of the year you have $1200 in the bank, waiting for the rainy day when something goes wrong, or for the sunny day when you need to put a down payment on a house or car, or to start a business.

Attainable

I truly believe the sky is the limit when you set goals for yourself. The only thing holding you back is usually your own inaction, usually brought on by fear or lack of belief in yourself. That being said, there are limits. I am never going to fly to the moon without a spacecraft. I am never going to walk all the way around the equator. I am never going to play pro football.

It is important that your goals are attainable, with a stretch. Going to work tomorrow isn't really a goal for me. I love where I work, but I am going there without having to set that goal. The goals that I set for myself have a little more meat to them. Losing 20 pounds is certainly attainable to me. I probably should lose 25. Saving $1200 a year is also attainable with a stretch. I am sure that I could make do on $25 less per week. Wouldn't always be fun, but I could tighten the belt and do it.

Relevant

The goal must be relevant to the person setting it. If it is not relevant to you, you won't do it. I could set a goal of making sure my neighbor loses 20 pounds, but that goal isn't really for me; it's for him or her. The goal has to be important enough to me that I am willing to pay the price to achieve it.

The second part about relevant goes back to something I said earlier. Your goals cannot be in conflict with your values and roles. If I owned a factory, increasing production by 25% by demanding everyone work more hours would be in direct violation of my value that family is first. I would be requiring my employees to be away from their families so that I could profit. If, however, I were to give people the choice to work more hours, maybe to earn more money for Christmas shopping, that would not be in conflict with my values. In fact, it would be a situation that could benefit both sides. Those are the best solutions.

Timely

No goal will work if you don't put a time frame on it. If you don't have a deadline, then you have nothing to measure against. "I want to lose 20 pounds by our vacation in April" is a goal with a very definite end on it. Just saying "I want to lose 20 pounds" is fuzzy, and as we've seen, fuzzy goals don't get realized.

The most effective way to achieve your goals is to make sure that you clearly understand them. Goals that are specific, measurable, attainable, relevant and timely have a much better chance of being successful. When you have all of those SMART elements of a goal working together, you have a much clearer picture of exactly what price you will have to pay to reach your goal. And if you know the price, you can decide if it is worth it.

Committing To Your Goals

The next step on the road to reaching your goals is to commit to them. There are a couple of ways to do this. The first, and possibly the most important, is to write them down. There is something about writing a goal down that makes it seem more serious.

I'm not talking about writing them down on a napkin, or scribbling them somewhere in the back of a notebook or yellow pad where you will probably never see them again. I am talking about writing them down and putting them in a place where you can see them often.

Some people put their goals in a diary or journal. Others post them on the mirror in their room so that they see them every day when they comb their hair. The *where* is only important in so much as they are someplace that you can see them every day to remind yourself. The dashboard of your car, inside your locker, near your desk. Any of those will work. My life is filled with reminders of things in places where I need the trigger. One of the best teachers I have ever known passed away a few years ago. I have her picture posted to the wall above my desk to remind me that I should work hard to be the best teacher that I can. I have ticket stubs from a Broadway play that I loved stuck to the wall above my desk at home to remind me to work hard so that I have money to play hard. My goals, however, are written down in my daily planner, which I carry with me almost everywhere, and I look at it many times throughout the day. My goals are always in front of me.

Time Management

Time management is the process of scheduling your time so that you are using it efficiently and making sure you make space in your schedule for the things that are most important to you. If you are scheduling the tasks that will help you move closer to your goals, you are more likely to achieve them. Time management is also one of the key skills that college professors believe students are lacking when they arrive at (and sometimes when they leave) college.

One of the big keys to reaching your goals is to break them down into little bite-sized chunks. Getting up 12 feet in the air is much easier if you have a staircase of 12 steps that leads you up. Each step is an intermediate goal that will get you to the top. Stairs offer a chance for you to stop for a minute to catch your breath. Intermediate goals do the same thing. Once you reach your smaller goals you can stop and take a breather, if you choose, before moving on to tackle the next part of the next intermediate goal. It's a chance to rest, and like we discussed earlier, maybe reward yourself for your success. Rewarding yourself is a great technique to motivate you to reach a goal.

Here's the way it works. There are three phases in goal setting. The first phase is the long term, or ultimate goal. This is the big picture, the thing you want to achieve in the end. It can be a six months away, or a year away, or five years away. Very successful people tend to think about the future. That way they always have something that they are working towards.

The second phase is to break it down into chunks that are easy to swallow. Saving $10,000 in five years sounds pretty daunting. Saving $2000 per year for five years sounds much easier to do. If you are immediately frightened off by the sound of the long term goal, you are less likely to believe that you can do it. If you don't believe you can do it, you are right. Remember our conversation about the part of our mind that works subconsciously? If you can't talk that part of your mind into your goals, it will not be supportive and will allow your inner voice to work hard to sabotage your success. Breaking goals into more manageable and less intimidating chunks makes it easier to sell yourself on them.

The third phase of goal setting is to assign yourself even smaller daily tasks that will move you towards your intermediate goals. This is the nitty gritty, boots on the ground work. If you want to lose weight, you have to schedule the exercise time. You have to *actually* schedule it. You will walk on the treadmill for 30 minutes from 4pm – 4:30pm. If someone else wants to schedule something else, you have to say "No, I have something scheduled at that time". This is why it is important to write down the long-term goals to remind yourself, the medium term goals to track your progress, and the short term goals so that other people's priorities don't overtake your priorities. If something is a priority to you, schedule it.

There are so many ways to keep track of your appointments and task lists now. You can do it on your computer, you can do it on your smart phone, or you can do it on your tablet. I still love to write things down with old school pen and paper. I use a weekly planner that allows me to keep track of my daily appointments as well as making a daily task list. It took me a few years of trying different planners before I settled on the one I use, and now I have created a system around that particular planner that works pretty well for me.

You'll have to decide what system works best for you. Don't be afraid to use it in a way that it wasn't originally meant to be used if that will make it work better for you. My planner has a space for each day of the week, and then one generic box to fill out the week. I draw a line down the middle of each daily box. On the left side I write my daily appointments because there are times printed there. On the right side I make a list of the tasks I have to do each day. Once they are done, I check them off. I love to see check marks because they represent my progress. I use the generic box to put my weekly goals in it.

Does it sound like a lot of work? It really only takes me minutes each day. At the beginning of the year, I spend a little more time planning out the year. At the beginning of the month, I look at things I have to achieve in the next thirty days. So, maybe it takes me an hour in late December or early January, and maybe it takes me a half hour at the beginning of each month. Can't you find 7 hours A YEAR, plus a couple of minutes a day to make sure you are seeing your goals clearly, and working towards them?

The 80-20 Rule

The biggest benefit to writing things down is that you get to look at all of the things you need to do and then you get to decide what is most important. The key is to look at the tasks at hand and to recognize which tasks will provide you the greatest benefit. The benefit, of course, means that completing the task moves you closer to your goals.

The 80-20 rule applies to lots of different things. In business it is said that 80% of the profits will come from 20% of the customers. Wouldn't it then make sense to focus more of your energy on the 20% of the customers that account for most of your business?

In organizations, 80% of your results come from 20% of the people. We have all been a part of a team or group at some point in our lives. It might be a sports team, or a business, or a community organization. Isn't there always a group of people that do most of the work? There's always a small percentage of people that take on the most work and responsibility, and ultimately they generate the most results.

In time management and goal setting, you will get 80% of your results from 20% of your actions. Think about all of the little things that you have to do each day. How many of them actually get you closer to your ultimate goals? Does washing the dishes help you achieve your ultimate goal? Does mowing the lawn? Does answering your e-mail every hour? These are all mundane tasks that we have to do throughout the course of our daily lives, but they really don't move us any closer to success. One could argue that they hinder success, as they get in the way of doing the tasks that will really get you moving forward. So, while those other little things need to get done, make sure that you schedule the 20% of the tasks that will reap the biggest rewards first.

Remember, that each and every one of us has a very different definition of success. Our individual definitions come from the values that we talked about earlier. If you value family time, then spending more time with your grandmother or your little brother and sister will be of much larger benefit to you than watching television alone. With so many methods of communication available today, there is no reason why you can't connect with your family frequently. Sometimes even a short text message means the world to a loved one, and making someone they love happy will benefit the family centric person. Schedule time to connect with your family and don't let other things encroach on that time.

Managing your time and scheduling your priorities does not mean you have to schedule every minute of your day. Nor does it mean that you cannot be spontaneous and have fun. What it does mean is that you need to put the things that are most important to you first on your list, and that you can't let other trivial things get in the way. It isn't that hard to do, but it is a habit that you will need to work on developing. Making a daily, weekly and monthly plan won't happen overnight. You'll have to commit to doing it, and you'll have to consciously make it happen. The benefits, however, will be worth it.

Chapter Five Highlights

- Everything has a price. If you are willing to pay it, you can achieve it.
- You have to visualize what you want to achieve clearly in your mind before you can move towards it.
- The goals you set need to be SMART goals – specific, measurable, attainable, relevant, and timely.
- The best way to commit to your goals is to write them down in a place you will see them frequently.
- Time management is the process of scheduling the tasks that get you closer to your goals. It helps you to use time more efficiently. It is also one of the skills that college professors see that students are lacking when they come to college.
- Break long-term goals into smaller chunks to make them easier to achieve.
- You will get 80% of your results from 20% of your actions, so you need to prioritize and put that most fruitful 20% on the top of your "to do" list.
- Schedule the things that are highest priority to you and don't let trivial things encroach on them.

ACTIVITIES

Student Activities

- Think about one big thing you would like to achieve this year. Close your eyes and see it clearly in your imagination. See yourself enjoying the moment as you achieve it. Once you visualize it clearly, commit it to your memory and recall it every night before you go to bed. Then visualize it again each morning before you start your day.

- Write down three SMART goals for the year. Put them someplace where you will see them often…on your bedroom mirror, inside your locker door, in your calendar.
- Break down each goal into smaller steps that you need to do to get to your big goal. **WRITE THEM DOWN**.

Teacher Activities

- Lead the kids in visualization exercises. Have them close their eyes and see themselves being successful on key assessments in your class.
- Set goals for yourself and your class at the beginning of the school year. Share those goals with the kids. Use your kids to hold you accountable. Make it a team effort. When you achieve one of your agreed upon milestones, reward yourself and the kids. Healthy snacks or a fun activity that they really enjoy are good rewards.

Parent Activities

- Make family goals. Use each other to hold each other accountable. Save for a trip. Do a long-term project together. Reward yourselves for reaching milestones. Maybe a movie or nice family night out.
- Share some of your adult goals with your kids and tell them what you are doing to reach them. They are going to have to set adult goals for themselves someday. Teach them about them. They will learn from you. If you set goals they will learn that. If you don't, then that is what they will learn.
- Encourage your kids to set higher goals; to stretch themselves in order to reach things that are beyond what they thought they were capable of.

CHAPTER SIX
IT'S WHAT YOU KNOW <u>AND</u> WHO YOU KNOW

"Our greatest joy and our greatest pain comes in our relationships with others"
- Dr. Stephen R. Covey, author

The old saying "it's not what you know, it's who you know" is actually meant to illustrate that you can get a job without knowing the required material, so long as you know the right people. There is no doubt this is absolutely true. If you know the right person, or have the right name to drop, it can certainly help you advance in life. You see this frequently in politics and business, and I would definitely argue that if you want to be really successful, you should do your best to know all that you can about the job, as well as building a strong network of people.

What the old saying really illustrates is the power of the people in your life.

Relationships

Each and every one of us has relationships in our life. As we illustrated earlier by defining our roles, we are firmly connected to people. Whether it is our family, friends, or colleagues, people surround us and help to make us what we are, by loving us, supporting us, teaching us and sharing with us.

I am definitely the person that I am as a result of the things I have learned from the people in my life. Some of those lessons came from my family, others came from my friends, and many of the lessons came from my students. Yes, I learn as much from them as they hopefully do from me.

While many people define themselves by what they do and what they have acquired, many others define themselves by the relationships they have. My most cherished things in life aren't my bank accounts or my cars, they are my relationships with my family and friends. Those people bring me the most joy in life. Most often, when I choose to spend money it is on things that I can do with or for my family and friends.

I once had a conversation with a friend of mine who is a pretty successful guy. He is very smart and very good at business. He knows how to see opportunities and turn them into money. On the other hand, he has never been married or had any children. One day when we were together with a whole group of our friends, he told me that he knew some of us envied him for his success and its rewards. It's true, I wish I could travel the world whenever I wanted to like he does. He went on to share that he envies us for our nice families and the rewards that come with that. He has worked very hard in his life. Not one ounce of his success was just handed to him. Yet, at the end of the day, he doesn't have anyone to come home to and share the stories of his day with. Clear proof that we all measure success by different standards.

Do not misunderstand me. Financial success and wealth are wonderful. It is great to work hard and to then see the fruits of that labor. Another old saying is that "money can't buy happiness", and that's true as well. However, having money sure helps take the stresses out of daily life. It is not an easy or happy life when you have to worry about paying the rent or putting food on the table. Money, in and of itself is just a tool. Real happiness comes from having rich and rewarding relationships in your life. You absolutely can have both money and really strong relationships. You can also live a very happy life that is financially modest. It's just a matter of putting all of those things in perspective.

The Maturity Continuum

In the very first part of Chapter One I discussed the Maturity Continuum, as Dr. Stephen Covey describes in "The Seven Habits of Highly Effective People". As we talk about relationships, it bears repeating.

As we age, we naturally go through certain stages of maturity. In the first stage, we are *dependent* on people for everything. We can't walk or talk. We can't feed ourselves or cloth ourselves. In the earliest years we can't do anything for ourselves. Our family teaches us the very things that we need to do to survive. Some things we learn on our own, like the unpleasant effects of touching hot stoves or tasting things that are icky. Primarily though, we need the guidance of other people in our lives.

The second stage of maturity usually comes in the high school years. It is *independence*. We can do things on our own, and we crave being out from under our parents' control. We want people to stop telling us what time to come home, or what movies we can watch, or how much time we can spend on the phone. We want to pick out our own clothes and choose our own friends. If you act maturely, hopefully your parents recognize that and allow you some freedom.

The final stage of maturity is *interdependence*. This is the stage that hopefully we all reach, but more importantly, we all hopefully recognize how wonderful interdependence is. In the interdependent stage, we need each other. We enjoy the relationship of give and take. We relish in the moments when we can help those we love when they are in need, and we are comforted by their help when we need it most. It is these interdependent relationships that make our life full and rewarding. There is nothing I love more than hearing of my son's or my wife's accomplishments. I love to hug them or high-five them when any of us succeed. And my accomplishments feel even bigger when I know that they are proud of me.

In regards to money, as a family we do OK. We are

hard workers and we are rewarded for our efforts and our expertise. We don't live in a mansion or have expensive cars in the driveway. What we do with our extra money is take family vacations each year. The best memories in my life always involve someone I love. We like to spend our money on creating memories with each other.

Interdependence allows for people to share each other's experiences and expertise. It is a state of working together, and it makes challenges easier. It is very rewarding to have people you can share with in both emotional and physical tasks.

Trust

Remember how in the last chapter on goals I said that everything has its price? Well, the price tag on great, fulfilling relationships is trust. It's the absolute foundation on which any good relationship is built. There can be no strong relationship between family, friends or co-workers that doesn't involve trust.

Trust is definitely a two-way street. Both people in a relationship have to work towards it each and every day. If they don't, the relationship will not be strong. It just won't flourish.

The thing about trust is that it is extremely difficult to build, but it is very easy to destroy. It's kind of like building a large wall. It takes a long time to stack all of the bricks just right, but it doesn't take long to push the whole wall over. Then you have to start over again stacking the bricks back up again. First, however, you have to clear away the wreckage of the fallen bricks to make room to start over. Forgiveness takes time and it is often a difficult and painful process.

How do we build and maintain trusting relationships? First and foremost, we need to be honest. Honesty can be difficult. Sometimes we fear the consequences of something we've done, or haven't done. Sometimes we just don't want to hurt the person. Sometimes we are just being selfish. Sometimes we want to be accepted, so we make up stories about ourselves. In the end, when the person you are trying to impress learns of your storytelling, you end up having exactly the opposite effect that you were looking for. There is nothing that will push over that wall of trust faster than dishonesty.

Everyone has probably heard this before, but the truth is always the best approach, for multiple reasons. First, you never have to try and remember what the truth was. It is in your mind, and if you tell the truth you will remember it. If you tell a lie, it is not as easy to remember and often you will slip up later because you don't remember what you said. The truth will always be there.

The second great thing about the truth is it shows that you are a responsible person. We will all make mistakes. I make them every day. I am not afraid to own my mistakes. If I make one, I take responsibility for it. Mistakes are a great way to learn. If you pay attention to what happened, just like touching the hot stove when you are little, you can learn not to do that again. No one is perfect. Learn from your mistakes and take honest responsibility for them. If you are willing to say honestly, "Yes, I did that, and I am sorry. I learned my lesson and it won't happen again". And here's the important part, "How can I make it up to you?" If you are willing to do that, you can maintain your trusting relationship, even when things go wrong.

Similarly, blaming someone else is a good way to lose trust. If something bad happens and you find every other person to blame it on, you will lose trust quickly. In a bad situation, don't look for a place to put the blame, look for a solution to the problem instead. Asking "How can we fix it?" is a much better question than, "Who can we blame it on?" It shows that you are problem solver, not a blamer. Problem solvers earn trust. "It's not my fault," burns trust.

Another way to earn trust is to make sure the things

that are important to your loved ones, are also important to you. Remembering significant days like birthdays or anniversaries is easy and important. Making time for their needs or to recognize their accomplishments also helps to build up an emotional trust which strengthens relationships. It helps when other people know that they are important to you.

Doing more than the minimum requirement builds trust as well. It strengthens the relationship when people know that they can count on you. If you do just what it takes to get by, that shows you can't be trusted to take the steps needed for real success. This is just as important in interpersonal relationships as it is in relationships at work. Sometimes mom or dad are busy with work or with your siblings. If they have to beg to get the garbage taken out, or the laundry folded, it doesn't instill trust that you are mature enough to recognize when things need doing. Showing initiative and taking on more responsibilities that weren't necessarily delegated to you really builds trust. This is true at home, at school, and at work. It shows that you are invested in the relationship.

Things that you may think are silly can have an impact on the trust in your relationships. Not dressing nicely for an event that is important to someone else can affect the trust in a relationship. Borrowing something without asking can also affect the trust in a relationship. Obviously, things like being late or not showing up at all, can deeply damage trusting relationships. People need to know they can count on you. They need to know they can count on you to do what is required. They need to know they can count on you to do the right thing. They need to know they can count on you to be where you are supposed to be, when you are supposed to be there. It shows them you recognize that their time is just as important as yours.

Finally, one of the biggest killers of trust is when you say that you will do something, and then don't live up to that promise. Here's an important tip: don't say you will do it if you won't do it. If you commit to something, get it done.

There is no stronger element of a relationship than trust. It is hard to build and easy to destroy. Trust is like a plant. It continues to grow, and it grows better when it is nurtured. When it is not tended to, it withers and dies. Work hard to nurture relationships filled with trust in your life.

You Can't Choose Your Family, But You Can Choose Your Friends, So Do it Carefully

Most times, we tend to choose our friends by our geographic connection with them. Whom we sit next to in school or with whom we work. I have people in my life that I felt like we were good friends when we saw each other at work each day. We would eat lunch together, go out after work, and maybe even get together on our days off. After one of the two of us moved to a different job, the relationship faded. Now we see each other by bumping into each other in the mall or maybe we get together once a year. It seems like once we didn't see each other 4 or 5 days a week, there was nothing left to build that relationship on. The same thing can happen when you move away from one neighborhood to another.

There are, of course, exceptions to that rule. We graduate from high school or college and move on to the next chapter of our lives, but there are still 5 or so really good friends that we keep in touch with. I have a group of close friends from high school and we try to get together a few times a year, just to catch up. Life gets busy, but you will always have your closest friends to turn to.

The second way we choose our friends is by common interest. We make friends on the sports field, or in the band, or in the Environmental Club, with whom we have a common bond. We like the same things, which is the bond that holds us together.

Both of those methods make it seem as though choosing our friends is left to luck and to fate. To a certain extent, being in the same place together at the same time is a bit of luck. We, however, have a choice whether to invest in those friendships and help them to grow.

Who your friends are is very important. They have a continuous and lasting effect on your life. First, they help to shape your behavior. If you hang out with people who are not very nice, you will absolutely adopt those negative characteristics. Bullies usually have a crowd of followers that stand behind them and support their taunting of others. Look around you; don't the gossipy people tend to find each other? Then they can all sit around and gossip together.

Conversely, when people who have strong, positive character traits form a group, they amplify those things. They help each other out, and that raises the level of the entire group. Maybe they do community service or study together. Maybe they stand up for the people who others put down. Even a small group of good people becomes a strong force of good.

"You are who you associate with. Look at your five closest friends and that's who you are. If you don't want to be that person, you know what you have to do."

– Will Smith, actor

This is why it is very important for you to choose your friends carefully. You certainly can accept geographic or incidental selection of friends, or you can proactively look for people to make friends with who will constantly challenge you to be a better person.

When my son, Adam was in middle school, he was kind of shy and reserved. He was involved in the school bands, but he wasn't involved in much else at that school. He didn't have many friends that he hung out with after school. He was kind of a loner. He was also experiencing academic difficulties. His grades were much lower than he was capable of achieving.

As a family, we decided that for high school Adam would move to the smaller, private school where I work. In the smaller environment, Adam began to make friends, and he also started to get involved with school activities. He was elected to the Student Senate and he got involved in the Stage Crew. His grades started to improve.

The next year, as a family, we talked again and we decided that, even though his grades weren't high honors, he should challenge himself and take some Advanced Placement classes. There were people who raised their eyebrows at our decision, but I believe pretty strongly in the idea of positive role models. The kids that I knew in those AP classes were not only good students, they were good kids. As Adam started to make friends in these upper level classes, his grades continued to rise. By the time he graduated, he was on the honor roll. I cannot think of 8 nicer kids, and they certainly have had a very positive impact on Adam. As he continues on in life, Adam has shown a tendency to choose friends that are good, hardworking, passionate people, the kind of people that push Adam to achieve better things.

The other important consideration when choosing your friends is that they will absolutely have an impact on how other people view you. We talked earlier about the importance of your image. Your friends will have a definite impact on your image. If you hang out with people who are believed by others to be unethical, immoral, or unkind, those characteristics will be attributed to you as well. If you spend time with people whom others hold in high regard, they will usually believe that you are a person of character as well.

Your friends will play a very important role in your life. You should identify people who share the same positive values as yourself, or values that you would like to live by, and make an effort to become their friend. You will take on the characteristics of your group of friends, so choose friends who are well-respected and are good people, and who will challenge you to be better.

Negotiations

When we hear the word negotiations, we tend to think of big business deals. The truth is, we negotiate each and every day. We negotiate with our parents about our curfew or borrowing the car. We negotiate with our friends about what movie to see or where to eat out after school. We negotiate with our boss about which days we can work and which days we can take off. Once we realize that life is a series of negotiations, we can change the way that we act, and hopefully get more of the things that we want.

From a very young age, we are taught to believe that in every situation there needs to be a winner and a loser. We are a society that loves our sports, which further deepens our competitive spirit. I am writing this chapter on Super Bowl Sunday, and I spent the past week in a friendly taunting match with one of my college buddies who is rooting for the other team. People are competitive by nature.

Because of our competitive side, we believe that in order to win something, the other side needs to lose. When it comes to negotiations, that simply isn't true. Particularly when we are negotiating with someone we love and trust.

Negotiations are designed to be a "give and take" procedure. They don't have to be a "take as much as you can" event. In business, that is often the accepted model, but I absolutely don't believe that. If both parties were to enter negotiations believing they are there to make sure both sides leave the table happy, think of the things we could achieve.

Here's how to start. If we want something, we have to decide what price we are willing to pay for it. What would we be willing to give up in return? Let's say, for example, that I need some extra money. Instead of just asking my mom or my boss for extra money or for a raise, I could present the case by offering to do something more in order to earn the extra money. You could do an extra job around the house or offer to take on more responsibility at work in return for the extra cash. Both sides get something in that deal. Dr. Covey calls this "Think Win/Win" and it is Habit #4 in "The Seven Habits of Highly Effective People".

Let's say, for example, that you want to borrow the car to go out with your friends on Saturday. You could offer to drive your little brother or sister to and from their soccer practice for the rest of the week in return for the use of the car on the weekend, or you could offer to wash and wax the car. Both sides get something in that deal, and you came to the table showing that you didn't expect something for nothing.

Even in business, if one party walks away from the table feeling that they were slighted, it does nothing to maintain the good relationship between the two parties. If one party loses, resentment starts to build and the relationship will not be as fruitful going forward.

There is almost always a middle ground that can be reached. Regardless, of whether they can get all the way there, it should always be the goal of both parties at the negotiating table.

Networks

Networking used to be primarily a sales term, but each and every one of us has a life filled with networks. It is never too early or late in life to start to pay attention to your networks.

When Facebook was first invented, it was designed for college students to interact and get to know each other on their individual campuses. You had to list a school in order to sign up for Facebook.

When I look at my list of Facebook friends, they come from all different aspects of my life, all different networks. There are people with whom I grew up, people I went to high school with, and people I went to college with. Inside the "people I went to college with" network, there are my fraternity brothers and my theater friends. There is a network of people I have worked with in the past. There are people I work with now. There are students I have taught along the way. My life is made up of a series of different networks. All of these small networks make up my big overall network.

Networks are an incredibly important nowadays. I opened this chapter with the statement "it is not what you know, it is who you know". It is important that you are aware of your network and you carefully work to maintain it. You never know when you might need help with something. If you work hard to be an impressive person, through your words and deeds, your network will grow, and someone in your network will usually rise up when you are in need. Note the beginning of that sentence. "If you work hard to be an impressive person....". When people are impressed with you they are willing to take a chance on you, either by helping you out directly, or by recommending you to other people. Both of those things can help you achieve what you want in life. Your network is absolutely essential to your success.

A network doesn't just appear and grow. Like trust, it needs to be tended to and nurtured. I am a guy who likes to help people out. As a matter of fact, I like to think that helping people is central to my mission in life. I absolutely believe that if I help other people become successful, success will come to me. It's worked pretty well so far in my life. People that I have helped recommend me to other people. I don't advertise and I have gotten lots of work through word of mouth. Someone who I don't know will call me and say "Hey, I got your name from (fill in the blank). Do you still do (fill in the blank)?" Often that turns into paid work for me. I always call my friend who referred me and thank him or her for the referral, so that they know that I appreciate that they took time to recommend me. "Thank you" cards or emails are big part of network maintenance.

So, wherever you are in life right now, take a minute to look at your network. Who do you know? How are they connected to you? The cool thing about social media is that it makes it easier to stay connected with your network, no matter where they are. You can use social media as a tool to stay connected with your network.

Network Building

The more people you know, the better chances you have of finding people to help you with the things you need. It is important to actively build your network, not just let it grow on its own. Go to events that are of interest to you. Meet people. Build your network.

One of the frustrating things about a college education now is the expense. My son's tuition cost at a state college right now is about double what I paid for tuition, room, board, books and fees. I might have even had a little left over for some macaroni and cheese and Ramen noodles. And the thing is, I went to a private university.

The astronomical cost of college has forced a lot of kids to stay at home and commute to college. The problem is that commuters tend to treat college more like a job. They go for class, to use the library or lab, and then they go home. When you live in a dorm on campus, you have extra time, and you live right there, so you tend to get more involved in the extracurricular life on campus. You join fraternities or sororities, you join clubs, you go to speakers or panel discussions. More importantly, as a part of these activities, you meet people. These are the people who share your interests, and they will often turn out to be your life-long friends. They will also be the people who make up your network.

There are so many ways to met people and build your network. Here are just a few examples:

1. Volunteer for a political candidate you support.
2. Organize or attend a neighborhood or park clean-up.
3. Volunteer for a fundraiser or other charity event.
4. Chair a committee.
5. Join a group at your church.
6. Attend a conference or presentation.
7. Join a group dedicated to your hobby.
8. Attend a dedicated networking event.

No matter where you are in life, you can get involved in activities that are of interest to you, and you can start to make friends and build your network. I work on my network all the time.

Network Maintenance

A good friend of mine, Tony Moreno, is our computer network guy at school. He said to me once, "you don't get a stable network environment by crossing your fingers". Tony is constantly doing little computery things that I don't understand, to keep our network from crashing. Every time I turn on my computer, it goes on. Every time I look for my files, they are always there. That is all due, in part, to Tony's deliberate network maintenance.

Your network of people requires that same constant maintenance. You need to do small things like wish people a "Happy Birthday" or "Happy Retirement" or "Happy Anniversary". You need to take a minute to congratulate people on their accomplishments or tell them you feel sorry due to their loss of a loved one. You need to sing praises to them for doing something great, and especially for doing something for you.

The other thing that you need to do is help people in your network. If they need a favor and you can do it, then do it. If they are looking for an expert in something and you know one, connect them. If they are an expert in something and someone else is looking for something, refer them. These are all outstanding ways to maintain your network. I do a lot of favors for people. I don't expect anything in return. I like to help people. The truth is, however, people do give you things in return. They start to refer you to their network. They start to post congratulations about your accomplishments on their Facebook wall. They start to tell people how great you are. They are usually appreciative and they usually show it. When you give of yourself to others in your network, they often return the favor. You become known as a person who helps out. You become known as a person who is generous and gives. We'll talk more about it in a later chapter, but people who give of themselves usually get things that they want in return.

Communication

I really cannot stress enough the importance of good communication in a strong relationship. It is essential that you keep an open flow of information with your closest family and friends. It is equally important to communicate well with your co-workers and people you are partnering with on a project. There is nothing more damaging to a relationship than not knowing what is going on.

Communication involves a lot of different things. First and foremost, people do not like to be surprised, especially by bad news. We talked earlier about owning our mistakes, and taking responsibility for them. It is also important that we communicate our mistakes to the appropriate people. If I make a big mistake at work, I immediately tell the people above me who need to know about it. This way, if there are repercussions from the mistake, my bosses heard it from me first, not an angry parent or a vendor we do business with. If you believe there is no chance that anyone will find out about your mistake, you are probably wrong. Bad news travels fast. Go tell the people who need to know, and don't wait until it comes from another source. Be open and honest and do it immediately. Once they find out from someone else, the trust between you has been damaged. Maybe your trust will be damaged anyway, but if you communicate quickly, you may be able to lessen the damage to the trust.

Communicating your emotions is also important in a relationship. If someone hurts your feelings it is necessary to address it with them in a rational and mature way. There is absolutely nothing wrong with saying "you really hurt my feelings (or embarrassed me, or made me feel bad) when you said (fill in the blank)". Sometimes people are joking about something and don't realize that it hurt your feelings. Other times they take things out of context. Regardless of their intent, people who care about you would not want to intentionally hurt you. If they do hurt you let them know so they can avoid doing it again.

On the other hand, we might hurt someone we care about through a careless act or a poor choice of words. When we do that, if we truly care about them, an apology is required. If we know we hurt someone and we decide to let it slide, resentment begins to build. As resentment grows, it turns into an explosion and sometimes the end of a relationship. Sincerely apologizing is a difficult thing to do. Our defense mechanisms often make us think that apologizing will make us look weak. Nothing could be further from the truth. People who can sincerely apologize for some negative thing they have done or problem they have caused, show a self confidence which is strength, not weakness.

Communication also involves keeping people informed about your progress. If you are working on a group project, it is good for everyone in the group to check in with each other frequently so that everyone knows where everyone else stands. It is terrible when one person is floundering and the group doesn't know. If all members of the group know where each other stand, then a person who is falling behind can get assistance from others.

The importance of communication also relates to things like being late. If someone is expecting you at a certain time, it damages the trust others place in you if you arrive after the time you are expected. A simple phone call, e-mail, or text message can usually head this off.

Do you listen or do you hear?

Some people read the above title and say "listen or hear, what's the difference?" There is actually a pretty big difference. Hearing just happens. It is nothing more than sound being captured by the ear. As I sit here typing, birds are chirping, cars are driving by, and my dog is snoring. I hear them, but I am not listening to them.

Listening, on the other hand, is a conscious act that requires concentration and processing of the sounds that you hear. The conscious focus and processing leads to an understanding of the words and sentences, the tone in which they are said, and, ultimately, their meaning.

Often, as soon as a person starts to talk to us, we begin to craft our response. The minute that starts happening, we aren't really listening to them anymore. It is truly important to stop and listen to what the other person has to say. After you are done really listening, it is essential to take a minute to try and understand what they are saying.

Pay attention to what the other person is saying. Give them your attention, and show them that you are listening by nodding or adding short verbal cues. Most importantly, let them speak until they are done. Don't let your need to respond push you into interrupting them before they are done. This takes practice.

When they are done speaking, then you can provide your feedback, but only when they are done. The best personal and business relationships happen when people truly listen.

Relationships are two way streets. Both parties have to give of themselves and one of the best ways to show your commitment to the relationship is through good, honest communication.

Chapter Six Highlights

- The old adage, "It's not what you know, it's who you know" is true in more ways than one.
- Good strong relationships are what adds fulfillment to our lives.
- Interdependence is the highest state we can reach.
- Trust is absolutely the most important aspect of any relationship.
- Trust is like a stack of heavy bricks. It is hard to build up, and much easier to knock down.
- Choose your friends carefully. They shape your behavior and people will judge you based on them.
- When negotiating, look for a middle ground where both parties benefit.
- Even if we don't think about it, we all have a network of people that we start to build at a young age.
- Our networks require constant maintenance.
- Communication is key to good strong relationships. Good listening is key to communication.

ACTIVITIES

Student Activities

- Introduce yourself to at least one new person per week. Who knows, that person might turn out to be your best friend, your business partner or the love of your life.

- Make a list of important dates like birthdays or anniversaries and make sure you reach out to people on those days. Sometimes an unexpected good wish from someone makes a person's day.
- Practice listening. Look the person in the eye, smile and nod, and keep your mouth shut until they are truly done speaking.

Teacher Activities

- Don't always let kids work with their friends. Make them meet and get to know other kids in the class that they wouldn't normally work with.
- If someone outside of your class does something for your students, make sure that your group takes a minute to thank them.
- Post a list of all of your students' birthdays (or half birthdays if their actual date of birth falls during a vacation). Encourage kids to pay attention to the list and to proactively deliver birthday wishes to each other.

Parent Activities

- This is another chance to lead by example. Include your kids when you are building or maintaining your own network. Explain the things that you do to meet people.
- Actively listen to your kids. Let them finish speaking and don't judge immediately. If things aren't completely agreeable, see if you can offer a counter proposal. Don't watch TV or play a game when your kids are talking to you, and expect the same in return. No texting while a conversation is going on.

CHAPTER SEVEN
GIVERS GET

"If you want to lift yourself up, lift someone else up."
- Booker T. Washington, educator, author and orator

Every person on Earth has a unique situation. Some are wealthy, never wanting for a thing. Others have sleepless nights, trying to figure out how to put a meal on the table. While I would not call myself wealthy and never wanting for a thing, there is no question that I have been very blessed in life. For the majority of my life I have not had to worry about food or shelter. In the darkest moments when I did, my immediate family was surrounded by wonderful and generous extended family and friends who helped us through. They gave of themselves for us.

I grew up outside of Buffalo, NY, and while my parents weren't wealthy, we never really wanted for things. I don't remember being involved in community service or charity through my high school years. I do remember, however, my parents teaching me that there are always people in the world less fortunate than us, and that we should be thankful for the good things we had.

It was really when I got back to Buffalo after 4 years of college in Ohio that I started to learn about the joy of generosity and community service. A few things happened which made me start to pay attention.

The first thing was when I got a job. It did two things for me. It put money in my pocket, and it put me to work with groups of generous people. My first employers all supported the United Way. We could donate money through our paycheck, or more importantly to me, we could work on their annual "Day of Caring". The day of work was inspiring to me. Not only did we go out and provide labor for a great not-for-profit group that served persons with disabilities, but we got to tour the facility and see the good work they did. I honestly don't remember the name of the organization, but I remember how appreciative the clients were because we were there to help.

The second big thing that opened my eyes to the importance of charity and service is that I married my wife. Volunteerism is a huge part of who she is, and she taught me a great deal over the years. She volunteers regularly for community events and for not-for-profit organizations, and sometimes I go along to lend a hand. She volunteers for events through her work, or with her good friend, Patt Rozler, who is a truly amazing person when it comes to community service.

Patt is a born organizer. She also believes strongly that the many not-for-profit organizations in our area enhance our quality of life. She recognizes that all of these charity organizations are usually short on resources and need help to fulfill their missions. So, Patt formed a group of volunteers whom she calls on to work at these community events. These are all just people who realize how important it is to give back to their community. By getting a group together and tapping into that community spirit, Patt amplified their individual generosity. Groups of people, working together for a common good cause, can achieve amazing things.

The third thing that happened to me was awful. As I mentioned earlier, my 4 year old daughter was diagnosed with cancer. After a hard 21 month battle, cancer won. As horrific as this period of my life was, a lot of revelations came out of it for me.

In the initial stages of her disease, our life turned upside down. Emotionally, any sense of normalcy and routine was gone, and was replaced with indescribable fear. Financially, our world also changed drastically. I worked, while my wife essentially quit her job to spend the time tending to Rebecca's needs. She was only 4, and couldn't take care of herself. Very early on, we decided that she would never be left alone in the hospital. There were too many things said by doctors and nurses; there were too many tests; there were too many new procedures. Someone needed to be in charge. I learned quickly where my daughter got her courage. She learned it from her incredibly brave mother.

The toll the illness took on our family was enormous. Not only did we lose a huge part of our income, but we added some large expenses. The hospital was about 11 miles from our home. We sometimes made multiple trips a day. When you head off to the hospital, you never pack a lunch, so we were at the mercy of the hospital cafeteria and the local restaurants. There were additional costs for over the counter medicines that weren't covered by the health insurance. There were parking fees. It was crazy.

As part of the overwhelming confusion, I also felt as though we had just became charity cases. It was a huge blow to my pride, but an amazing thing happened. Our family and friends rose up to make sure that the money wasn't going to be an issue. I was astonished and humbled daily by the outpouring of support that we received. We never could have made it through that awful experience without those amazing people who surrounded us.

An unexpected consequence of all of this was that we were suddenly on the inside of a group of organizations that we had seen holding fundraisers in our community over the years. We met the people who spent their lives working to cure kids of cancer, and other debilitating diseases. We saw how things worked. And most importantly, we saw how these dedicated individuals threw everything they had at saving our daughter's life.

There were three primary organizations that worked tirelessly on our behalf. The first was the Women's and Children's Hospital of Buffalo. This is where Rebecca had her surgeries and went when she was having any adverse reactions to her chemotherapy treatments. I was born at that hospital, as were both Rebecca and Adam. Truthfully, I took it for granted until Rebecca's illness.

The second group was Roswell Park Cancer Institute, an internationally renowned cancer center that was right in my own backyard. This is where Rebecca received her chemotherapy and radiation treatments.

The third group was the Make-A-Wish Foundation of Western New York, who sent us on the trip of a lifetime to Disney World. The work that these groups do is always incredible and often heartbreaking, and when you are seeing it all from the inside and meeting all of these kids, you cannot help but wonder what you can do to make their lives just a little bit easier.

While my wife, Linda, was the primary caregiver during this period, I came to the hospital when I could to visit, or to give her a much needed break. I'd sit in the room with Rebecca until she got bored watching the Disney movies over and over and then I'd offer to push her around the halls in her wheelchair. The four year old would say things like, "Daddy, Natalia's mommy isn't here today, can we push her too?" Natalia was a little girl who was adopted from somewhere in South or Central America. Shortly after she arrived in the United States, she was diagnosed with a heart condition. Her parents lived much farther away than we did and her parents both had to work, so sometimes she would be left alone during the day. Next thing I knew, I was pushing two wheelchairs down the hall. It took my sick baby to point that out to me.

It was almost like these kids were all in the same class in school. Several kids were all diagnosed around the same time and we became a little family of our own. When we got to the hospital, we would check to see who was in. We talked and played games and ate together. After Rebecca died, I knew that I would never be the same. I am now incapable of seeing a kid in need without being moved, and wondering what I can do to help.

The final thing that happened to me was right around the same time that Rebecca fell ill. I took a new job. At the time, I labored over the decision. I almost said no. For whatever reason, I decided it was the right move and I left the safety, and good pay and benefits of a large corporate retailer to take a job as a teacher at a small Catholic High School. I took it because I have my Bachelor's Degree in Theater and as part of the job I would be able to rebuild the school's declining Performing Arts program.

Interestingly, it wasn't the theater part of the job that opened my eyes. It was all of the community service and charity that went on in the school. Each student was required to do community service each of their four years. Each month there was a "dress down" day, with the money helping someone in need. There were countless "mitten and hat trees" or canned food drives. There were basketball tournaments to benefit local homeless shelters and talent shows to

> *"The best way to find yourself is to lose yourself in the service of others."*
>
> *– Mahatma Gandhi, activist*

raise money for kid's charities. It was overwhelming, and it was wonderful. It felt really good to be involved in so many projects and events that had the mission of helping people. It's still one of my favorite parts of my job.

After Rebecca died, I was a mess. I fell into a life that was filled with deep sadness and pain. I tried to ease the pain with alcohol. I generally started to drink when I got home from work, and didn't stop until I went to bed. Every single day. During that time I was not good at being a father. I was not good at being a husband. And I was not good at being a teacher.

My wife, on the other hand, focused her energy on healing by volunteering even more. She became a parent advocate, writing a proposal to the hospital on how to improve the devastating experience for other families going through what we did. She also worked on fundraisers for the two different hospitals. Her most important step, however, was to begin to seriously volunteer for the Make-A-Wish Foundation. She knew firsthand how powerful it was to grant wishes for those kids, and she wanted to be a part of it. She was so dedicated, and so good at it that in a short time they offered her a job doing what she loved.

My grieving and alcohol abuse went on for five years. Eventually, I was able to wake up and see that I had plenty to live for. Most importantly, raising my son who needed me now more than ever. I received enormous support from my family and friends and my co-workers and the kids at school, and I was able to get my feet back on the ground. While I am not a guy who believes that "every cloud has a silver lining", once I was able to start thinking straight again, I did find that I was able to make some positive changes in my life that included making sure that my life includes service and charity all the time. It actually is one of my greatest joys.

Gratitude

The story above is obviously sad. In the end, I could have gone one of two ways. I could have been angry and hurt my whole life. Eventually, that would have turned people off. Had I continued the self-destructive lifestyle, maybe I would have lost my job, or my family, or even my life.

Instead, I chose the other way. I chose to learn a few things from the terrible times and tried to focus on some positives. The most important positive I realized was that life can change in an instant and we need to be thankful for what we have. Even without Rebecca I have some very great things in my life.

I quickly learned who my friends were. I am thankful for them. I can never repay them with money for what they gave to us during that awful time, but none of them expect any repayment. I can, however, repay them by working to help people who are in need now, like we once were.

Despite Rebecca's loss, I still have a family unit that is very close. Families often fall apart after the loss of a loved one. Ours did not. I'm thankful for that and try to show my gratitude by working actively to make the world a better place.

What I learned is that there are always people out there who have it worse than I do. If I can do something, however small, to show my gratitude for the great things which have happened to me in life, then I am going to do that.

Little Things Make a Big Difference

Over the years what I found is that my acts of service or charity don't have to be monumental endeavors. I don't have to raise a million dollars to build a new wing at the hospital. If I give ten dollars, that's ten dollars more than they had. Ten dollar bills stack up pretty quickly when there are a lot of people giving them. In the end, to give ten dollars, I had to sacrifice a small pizza, but the hospital might eventually get a new wing, and I helped out. That is worth far more than a pizza that I probably didn't need anyway.

I like events involving lots of people who can each do small things within their means. I like canned food drives, or mitten trees or used clothes drives. Those three things cost me very little and make a huge impact on people who need help immediately. I like dropping a dollar in the red buckets at Christmas time. It is, after all, only a buck. I like when stores have buckets I can drop my change in after natural disasters like Hurricane Katrina or the Earthquake in Haiti. Both of those affected a very poor population that couldn't rebuild by themselves.

By giving lots of little donations, big things happen, and I feel as if this is the least I can do in order to show my gratitude for the all the great things that continually bless my life. It's like the movie "Pay It Forward" where the teacher, played by Kevin Spacey, challenges all of his kids to do something nice for someone else after they are the recipients of an act of kindness. If we all pay it forward, imagine what a great world this would be.

I have a good friend named Matt Carlucci, who was one of my students. One day Matt was playing flag football with another of his good friends, Joe Malczewski, and they came up with the idea for an organization that does nothing more than support the community. And so, the B-Team Buffalo was born. This group is a grassroots organization that cleans up neighborhoods and plants trees. They decorate a poor neighborhood for Christmas every year, at no cost to the homeowners. They provide the volunteer labor needed for the events that other charitable groups put together. These people just give, give, give of themselves, and that is their sole mission. What an wonderful group.

The Generosity Habit

Like anything else, if you do it often enough, a charitable life becomes a habit. I hardly even think before I reach in my pocket to toss some money into a collection bucket of some sort. I usually say "keep the change" when it comes time to buy a raffle ticket for a good cause. I do whatever I can. I know that I have a good life and that it could always be worse. I know that because it definitely was worse, and the community rallied around us. Giving back is the least I can do. Don't wait until something bad happens to you before you become generous. Even if nothing bad ever happens to you, the fulfillment you can get from helping the less fortunate is enormous.

Givers Get

I called this chapter "Givers Get", because one of the remarkable byproducts of a life of service and charity is that we tend to get things in return. It should not be your motivation for doing charitable deeds, but there is usually an unexpected reward. People are impressed by generous people, and they will usually tell other people about you. Who knows what opportunities will arise from that. Since I started doing more charity and community service work, a world of opportunities has opened up for me. I've been asked to participate with other charitable groups, and I've been invited to sit on the Board of Directors of others. By volunteering and meeting and impressing people, others recognized that I was valuable and they wanted me to bring my ideas to their groups, and that is an exciting and gratifying feeling.

When you are generous and give of yourself, people notice. If you are in business, being generous may lead to additional sales. People really like doing business with community-minded people and businesses.

As an individual, when you are generous it enhances your image. By volunteering you will get to meet new people, and you will be able to build your personal network. We've already discussed how incredibly important it is to build and then continually maintain your network.

"No one has ever become poor by giving."

– Anne Frank, author and Holocaust

I don't ever do my charity or volunteer work because of these things I might get in return, nor do I expect anything. I do charitable acts because it is the right thing to do, and because I enjoy helping to make my community a better place to live. Good things do happen to me as a result of my charitable work. I get to meet new people, and I get exposure. Both of those things often reap further rewards.

What little acts can you do today to start making the world a better place?

Chapter Seven Highlights

- Givers get.
- Little acts add up and big things get done.
- Being generous and offering service is an excellent way to show gratitude for the things that you have in life.
- Being generous is a habit, like many other positive characteristics.
- When you get up and act, you will meet new people and do new things.

ACTIVITIES

Student Activities

- Volunteer for at least 5 things per year. They don't have to be big things. Go and read to some younger kids. Help coach a youth sports team. Shovel an elderly person's driveway in the winter. You can also contact a not-for-profit organization dedicated to some cause that has touched your life. These groups are always looking for help.
- Pick a dollar amount that you can afford. Maybe $2 or $5 a month. It doesn't have to be a lot. Give it to your favorite charity or charities. Whatever you can give is helpful to them.

Teacher Activities

- Discuss with your students any fun or exciting community service or charity events in which you have recently participated. This is great leadership by example. Tell them what it meant to you and to the people you served.
- Organize a class community service project. It can be something simple like a penny war between your classes, or even have the kids drop change they find on the floor, at school and at home, in a jar and donate it at the end of the year to a charity of their choosing. Lynn Leonard, a good friend and teaching mentor of mine, has raised thousands of dollars for "Habitat for Humanity" by picking up loose change off the floor at school.

Parent Activities

- Have a family charity each year. You can go serve them or you can save money together and make a donation.
- Talk to your kids about any charities you support.

CHAPTER EIGHT
YOU HAVE TO BLOW YOUR OWN HORN

"Talent is never enough"
– John C. Maxwell, author, speaker and leadership expert

The world changed. It used to be that you went to high school, and then you made a choice. You went to college, the military, or to work. While those three choices are still there, the conceptions and expectations on each have changed.

When I was in high school in the late 1970's and early 1980's, I was part of the first generation where going to college was the expected path. Before, that it was very common for people to finish high school and go directly into the job market. The United States, at the time, had an economy based on manufacturing. The technology industry was in its infancy, as computers hadn't found their place in homes and offices yet. The military was still a relatively low-tech "boots on the ground" organization, and the training opportunities offered were nothing like what is available today.

There was never a question of whether I would go to college. I was going, and the vast majority of my friends went to college as well. What no one recognized at the time was that we were in the beginning of a shift in the entire economic structure of our country, and higher education was necessary for the shift to happen.

Manufacturing to Information

A few things happened during the years I was in high school and on into my college years that changed the face of America forever. The first of these important shifts was set in motion in 1976 when a couple of nerds from California named Steve Jobs and Steve Wozniak invented the first computer for home use. There is no doubt in my mind that the microcomputer was the most important invention in the history of mankind. It changed everything.

The second monumental event was the election of Ronald Reagan as President of the United States. While Reagan is credited with many things, his most important accomplishment, in my opinion, was the end of the Cold War. It isn't that he won it and that our archenemy, the Soviet Union, collapsed that is important. It is how he won it that forever changed the way we do business in this country.

Reagan became single-minded in his desire to end the Cold War. Ultimately, he did it by growing our military development program exponentially. He threw gobs of money at the infant technology industry and had them design the biggest and the best weapons. They ramped up our production of nuclear armaments, but not more of the same ones that they had been producing. They created newer weapons that relied on the latest, greatest technology and which went boom better, or with more precision, and from farther away.

What drove all of these new weapons? Computers. The technology industry became the very model of innovation. Each new weapon required stronger computing power and more compact size. As quickly as new technology became available for military applications, old technology became obsolete and was then turned into devices which could be sold to nonmilitary businesses and to homeowners.

Ultimately, what we got out of all of this was small desktop computers and computer networks, and eventually the Internet. Then we got personal devices like cell phones and personal GPS and satellite radio. The electronics that were invented for military use allowed for the creation of robotics, which eventually found a place in our factories, lowering the number of workers needed, and in many cases, increasing productivity.

Offices became more high tech, and businesses sprung up around developing more technology products. As the industry grew rapidly, the need for workers in factories declined. Conversely, the need for college-educated people grew.

We have evolved from a nation in which the products that we made drove the economy, into a nation where information is the most important thing. Once we started that shift, it required a more educated population. That is why college has become so important. In the 1940's, 50's and 60's, we made our money off of our physical work in factories. Now we are changing to a society that makes a living using our minds.

As the world changed, we have been forced to change our way of thinking about how we will make a wage. All three of the choices I mentioned above … work, military, and college … have changed drastically. The straight to work path is much harder. Because so many people are going to college, it makes it much more difficult for someone without a college degree to compete. There will always be jobs for people in the service industries. There will always be a need for people to do the hard physical work and skilled trades that built our country. The difference is that with the manufacturing plants becoming increasingly high-tech, there is more of a need for educated people to work the machines. Don't get me wrong. It is certainly possible for people with only a high school education to make a living in the new high-tech world. It's just more difficult.

The military changed as well. It used to be that the majority of people went into the service and learned how to be combat personnel. The military is always on the forefront of technology innovation. With all of the high-tech equipment that the military uses, there is a huge need to train people to use the technology. We are fighting wars more efficiently and with less loss of life with all of the new technology.

Finally, the college option has changed as well. There are hundreds of new programs that did not exist in the 1980s to train people to work in our incredibly advanced society. Because college is much more of a necessity than it was before, the cost has skyrocketed. When I went to a very well respected private university in the 1980s the cost averaged around $8000 per year for the entire package – tuition, room, board and fees. The same college experience today costs over $45,000 per year at colleges all over the country.

What does any of this have to do with blowing your own horn? Everything. The modern world is much more competitive, and you have stand out if you want to be noticed.

Your Image, Your Brand

In Chapter Three we talked about your image. Each and every one of us has an image. As I said earlier, in the business world it is called a brand, and it is very well thought out. A company brand is controlled to make sure that decisions are made to enhance it, not hurt it, and it is fiercely protected. Your brand is created by the choices you make. Any choices you make reflect who you really are, and who you are perceived to be by others.

This chapter is essentially about marketing ourselves. This is definitely a subject that is not taught in high school. No one ever thinks of their personal brand like that. Conventional wisdom is that you market products and businesses, you don't market yourself, but that is incorrect. All of the same principles of marketing businesses and products apply to making sure that **you** stand out in the crowd. The world we live in is incredibly competitive now and it is essential that you work hard to make yourself stand out in the crowd.

Your Message

In past chapters, we talked about your values and morals, we talked about your image, we talked about your mission, and we talked about your networks. Those are the primary ingredients of a good personal marketing plan.

As we move forward with this chapter, let's be clear that I am not talking about putting up billboards with your picture on it, making radio or TV commercials for yourself, or taking out full page ads in the local newspaper. I am talking about being assertive about yourself in a way that does not paint you as a conceited or self-centered. It is simply about focusing on what you want in life, and looking for opportunities to present yourself as a candidate for those things that you desire.

"My life is my message."

– Mahatma Gandhi, activist

In advertising products and businesses, the starting point is the message. Product A tastes better than Product B. Business A is less expensive than Business B. Our product is healthier, or faster, or more necessary. The messages that are crafted for all of these ad campaigns are extremely well thought out, and carefully designed to make a personal connection with the person in charge of making the buying decision. Craft the message about who you are and what you represent in the same well thought out way. In order for you to get noticed, you have to make the choice that you are going to actively promote yourself. What you are going to actively promote is a message about you that is positive and makes a personal connection with the people you are trying to reach – for the college you want to get into, for the job that you want, for the idea you are trying to promote. You have to get the message out that you are worthwhile.

Communication Skills

I tell my students at school all the time that the most important thing they can learn in life is communication skills. This is another of the skills that college professors feel that high school students are lacking when they arrive at college. I cannot overstate the importance of good writing and speaking skills in this new, highly competitive economy we live in. If you want to succeed, you need to learn how to share your ideas effectively. A few paragraphs ago I was telling you how we are now in the Information Age. Research is easy. You need statistics to prove your point? You can go to the internet. You need an expert to back you up? Go to the internet and find out what experts say. Since information is readily available to almost everyone now, it is the presentation of the information that sets you apart.

> *"If I went back to college again, I'd concentrate on two areas: learning to write and learning to speak before an audience. Nothing in life is more important than the ability to communicate effectively."*
>
> *– President Gerald Ford*

The two most important skills to learn are writing and speaking. If you are able to do those two things, you are light years ahead of the competition. Let me say that again. The two most important skills to learn are writing and speaking, because these are the ways that you will share your ideas with other people. Do it well, and you will undoubtedly benefit. The best way to get better at either of these things is to look at how other successful people do it. If you want to be a better writer, be a better reader. I always have multiple books on a variety of topics that I am reading at any given time. If you want to learn to speak well, or better yet, present well, go to the internet and watch other people's presentations. With the advent of YouTube there are countless presentations on different topics. You can watch videos on anything. I recommend the TED Talks if you want to watch really good speaking and expand your mind at the same time. They add more video content every time there is a conference. You can find great presentations on almost any topic at www.ted.com .

The other great thing about learning these skills is that, is it is never too late to start improving at either one. You can start today whether you are 16 or 46 or 76.

Be Creative

Years ago, when searching for a job, we typed up our resume and cover letter, we tossed it into the mail, and we followed up a week later with a phone call. We were taught to be pretty bland. Resumes and cover letters were in black ink (because typewriters only did black and red) on plain white paper. Boring.

Nowadays, you have the whole world of creativity at your finger tips. You can add photos, you can use multiple fonts, you can use different colors. I am not implying that your resume should look like a poster for the circus. (Unless, of course, you are applying for a job at the circus, then you should definitely circus it up.) My point is that you have the technology to do some very interesting things. As long as it is tasteful, looks professional and is easy for the person reviewing it to get to the important information, go for it. Make yours stand out in the pile. Sometimes, I read a hundred resumes a year. The ones that appear amateur and look like not much effort went into them don't even get a full read, much less a call for an interview. The ones that look cool always get read cover to cover. If you don't have the skills, ask someone who does to help you out and then do something for them in return, which might just include paying them. There are lots of great books and websites out there that can help you create a dynamic resume that gets noticed.

Here's a few fun examples of some creative ways of getting people's attention. One of my friends, Brendan McDaniels, was applying for a job as a play by play announcer for a professional hockey team. Instead of a standard cover letter, he did a "Top Ten Reasons You Should Hire Me", modeled after David Letterman's famous bit. Some of his reasons were serious and some were fun. My son did the same thing for an on campus job that was listed as "no longer accepting applications". He ended up getting a call back about the job.

I once received a sales package from a company that had a small giveaway item inside the envelope. Normally I throw a lot of sales materials away without even opening them, but because this package had a surprise inside, I opened it. It had a package of peanuts in it, and said something like, "You'd be nuts not to take advantage of this offer". I have no idea what the product was, but because of the creativity, I still remember it all these years later.

One art teacher who applied for a job opening put in a small print of one of her paintings that was suitable for framing. I not only got to see her artwork, I got to decorate my office. She got an interview.

With the technology available today you can do all sorts of cool things. You can create a video resume or make a movie and post it on YouTube. Create a podcast that you can post that sounds like a newscaster reporting on you.

The point is that there is room for creativity in self-promotion these days. While you wouldn't want to replace the traditional resume, you can certainly use creativity to supplement it. With today's technology there is no excuse for a poorly constructed, unprofessional looking resume package.

Be Assertive

The second part of the equation is that you have to keep your eyes open for opportunities. I am constantly listening for potential ways for me to get the things I want. That might sound like I am an opportunist, but I am never looking for ways to take advantage of people. I like doing the different things I know how to do. I like helping people get better at public speaking. I like writing. I like social media. So, when I hear of someone who might need one of those things, I say something like "Hey, if you need any help with your social media, let me know. I'll take a look at it for you." It's a way to start a conversation, and that gives you the opportunity to prove that you are the right person for the job.

Hockey great, Wayne Gretsky is famous for saying "You miss 100% of the shots you don't take". This is taking shots. The worst anyone can say is "no". My approach is to be assertive without being annoying. I mention it once and let it go. I am always surprised by how often I get a call back. There are two reasons I get the calls. First, and foremost, because I asked. Had I not said anything, they might not have connected me with what they need. Secondly, because I have impressed them in some other way, my personal brand is good to them, and they like me enough to trust me with their work. There needs to be a personal connection. I try hard to create as many personal connections as I can. I try to meet as many people as I can, and I try to impress as many people as I can.

The last part of being assertive is follow through. If you get someone to call you back, or ask for information, or you get your resume in the right hands, you have to follow through. It is easy nowadays. An e-mail or text, thanking them for seeing you or asking when you can set up a meeting, is a great start. If you submit a resume, call or stop by to see if you can set up an interview. It is harder to tell you no if they are looking at you or can hear the sound of your voice, and it is much easier to ignore a digital message.

Again, you have to balance between showing initiative and having a restraining order filed against you for creepy stalking.

Social Media

It is so much easier to market yourself today than ever before. While the "social" in social media implies a use that is not about business, it is a perfect way to reconnect with old friends, make new friends, and to grow your personal network. It's also a way to impress people.

Like everything else in this book, your social media use is a choice. You can use it to support a positive image of yourself, or you can use it to damage your reputation. The things you post on your social media pages give people an insight as to who it is you really are. If they see generally positive content on your site, they will believe that you are a positive and inspiring person. If you constantly post images of yourself doing inappropriate things, that is the image that will stick in their minds. You have to control the content that you put up there for people to see. People look at your social media, and potential employers will look at it, even for internships.

If you are younger, it may be difficult to see the importance of this. Social media is there for fun, right? You can absolutely have fun and post content that is likely to help you achieve the things that you want in life. Think about these different images. Who would you rather hire? You look at pictures of a couple of candidates on Facebook and the first one has pictures of your potential employee chugging drinks at a college party. The second candidate has pictures of the time that she spent a whole Saturday planting trees in a park. This is not to say that the second candidate doesn't go to parties, she just doesn't choose to advertise that part of her life in front of 800 million of her closest friends and potential employers. She recognizes that putting a positive image of herself out there supports the notion that she is a good person working towards positive things. In the end, do those party pictures do anything positive for you at all? The answer is no, but they absolutely **can** hurt you. They are a testament to your maturity and your values and they absolutely can sway someone's opinion against you.

If you think that your internet image doesn't matter, think again. Before you can be hired by some businesses, you have to provide a list of all of your social media outlets, blogs, or other online places where you express yourself. The people in charge of hiring are making sure that you are the type of person they want working for them. They want to make sure that you are not someone who will embarrass them or damage their image.

In addition to the pictures you post, the words and or links to other pages definitely say something about who you are as a person. If your online content is usually angry or critical, that says something about who you are. On the other hand, a person who posts positive or inspiring messages is someone that most people respect and enjoy following online. I link to news stories that are of interest to me. I congratulate people who have just done something awesome or achieved a milestone. I try to make people laugh. I want people to see a positive person when they look at my social media. I've said it before, nothing good ever comes from a negative thought or comment. Keep your image positive on your social media platforms, it will definitely yield positive rewards for you.

Once you have shown people that you are a generally positive influence, you can ask them things. I often turn to my social media to ask for suggestions for places to eat, to see if a new movie is any good, or to ask people's thoughts on a particular issue. The more friends that you have, the more likely you can get answers to your questions, get a good restaurant recommendation, learn about a cool opportunity learn about a cool opportunity or even uncover a tip for a job. The more opportunities of which you are aware, the more likely you will be able to take advantage of them.

While Facebook, Twitter and Google + are the more popular of social media, LinkedIn is gaining ground as the professional social media network. When the time comes to look for a job, a well thought out LinkedIn profile is a necessity for job hunting.

Another very important point, in this world of great access to information, is that one of the things potential employers do first is to Google your name. What will they find when they do? It is very difficult to hide negative stories in this world of 24/7 unlimited access. If you are a part of negative events, often that will show up when your name is searched. Keep an eye on that. Try it and see what shows up when you Google your own name.

Job Interviews

A thoughtful and sustained program of positive self-promotion will often get you in the door for opportunities you are pursuing. Whether a job interview or a sales call, face-to-face encounters are often underestimated. Potential employees get an opportunity to shine, while potential employers get to see how you act under pressure. I don't care how cool you are, everyone gets nervous and everyone is under pressure at a job interview. There is nothing fun about having to put yourself out there for evaluation. Here's some tips to help keep you as comfortable as possible:

Dress up - I don't care if you are applying for the lowest of the low jobs or a job in the executive corner office. Let the interviewer see that it is important to you. My first job interview was for a job mowing the lawns at a small advertising firm. I came running down the stairs in jeans and a tee shirt ready to go to the interview and my dad said "Where are you going? Get back upstairs and get yourself dressed for an interview". I went back upstairs and followed dad's advice and put on a shirt and tie. I was hired and the owner of the firm told me that it was because I dressed up and took the idea of the job seriously, even as a 16 year old kid. I am astonished at how many college graduates have no idea what a professional wardrobe is.

You don't have to go out and buy a fancy suit or dress. Wear something nice and take the time to put yourself together. Make sure all of your buttons are buttoned and your clothes are not dirty or wrinkled. Comb your hair, and brush your teeth. This may all sound elementary, but you would be surprised at how many people don't put time into their appearance before going to an interview. The effort that you put into making yourself look presentable is a direct reflection of what kind of employee you will be.

Do Your Homework – Whether you are applying to a company for the first time, or you have been called to come in for an interview, do some research about the company or even about the person interviewing you, if it is appropriate. Information is so easy to find. Even if a company doesn't have a website, they often show up in a Google search because of something they have done that was written about. If you can find out about a company's mission or their underlying values, you can tailor your answers to reflect those things. It never hurts in an interview to say "I saw on your website that you've won an award for best customer service in the area, I agree that the needs of the customers are the most important thing for a business." That sentence shows the interviewers two things. First, that you cared enough to put in some extra effort. Secondly, that you agree with one of the company's core philosophies.

"Fortune favors the prepared mind"

– Louis Pasteur, chemist and founder of Pasteurization

While you are doing your homework on the company, develop a list of questions that you can ask the interviewer.

Oftentimes the interviewer will ask you at one point or another if you have any questions. Saying "no" looks like you don't really care. If you properly do your homework, certainly some legitimate questions will come to mind. A question like, "If I got hired, would there be some sort of mentor program where I could learn things from employees who have been here awhile?" will earn you the respect of interviewers. Use the questions that you ask to show the interviewer that you are willing to learn, or that you want to know more about this company.

Follow through – This is a great piece of advice that you can use several times during the interview process. First, after you send the resume and cover letter, give it a week and if you haven't heard, give them a call. You can say things like "I was just calling to make sure you got my materials" or "I was wondering if I could set up an appointment to talk about my qualifications for the job".

After you have had your interview, again wait a few days to a week and follow through again. "I was wondering if there was anything else you needed from me to help in your decision." Both of these points of contact show the interviewer that you are excited and are willing to take initiative. Some people even send or leave cards thanking the people who interviewed them.

Give It Away

I think I have made it clear that it is a competitive world out there. You have to do what you can to give yourself an edge. Another method that is excellent for both you and the employer is when you offer to work for a short time for free. If you were to say, "I know you have a difficult decision to make in hiring. I would be willing to work for free for a week (or two or a month). That way I can learn the job and you can see what I will do for this company." It's like a short unpaid internship. Often, the offer alone will show the interviewer your level of commitment. This also works if you don't get the job, but are still interested in working for the company when another position opens up. My dad began his career emptying garbage cans in the office of a firm in which he eventually owned a share. Starting at the bottom can be a great place to begin.

If the company that you want to work for is one that relies on volunteers for any part of its operations, get in there and start volunteering. That is the perfect time to start impressing people. Remember earlier that I told you how my wife turned her volunteering at Make-A-Wish into a full-time job?

Companies often give free samples of their products to entice customers to buy. You can use the same philosophy and get your foot in the door by giving away some of your time for free.

Chapter Eight Highlights

- We are changing from a manufacturing society to an information society and that changes the kinds of education and skills we need.
- Technology changed everything.
- Businesses think hard about their image or brand. You should think hard about your brand too.
- Decide what it is that you want people to know about you. What is your message?
- Great communication skills will help you share your ideas well in writing or by speaking. This is important to your success and the skills you need are learned, so get going.
- Communication skills are an asset that college professors consistently note that high school kids are lacking.
- Everyone has a creative side. Tap yours to find ways to make you stand out in a crowd.

- You cannot get things if you don't actively pursue them. Be assertive and ask for the things you want. Worst thing they can say is "no".
- Social media offers a great way to communicate things about you. Be careful what you communicate because the social media audience is large and interconnected.
- For a good job interview you need to prepare. Dress up, research the company to formulate questions, and follow through. You will get noticed.
- Sometimes offering free samples is a great way to get your foot in the door of a company where you want to work. Be willing to volunteer in order to impress people.

ACTIVITIES

Student Activities

- Keep a running list of the activities that you are involved with and the dates that you did them. It will make writing your resume much easier when you need to do it.
- Avoid activities like gossiping or being hurtful. If malicious gossip is what you share or post, that is how people will view you.
- Post at least two positive things that you are involved with per week on your social media pages. Posts about charity events or other volunteer opportunities are great ways to showcase the good things you are doing. They are also good ways to advertise the events.

Teacher Activities

- Discuss how important it is to leave the negative thoughts and comments out of social media. Events at your school, and how the kids react, will often provide ample material to lead into this discussion.

- Take a few minutes to discuss positive activities in which your students are involved. Allow them to share their experiences in class.
- When appropriate, mention how hard it is to get rid of things that are posted on the internet. Also mention how fast things spread.

Parent Activities

- Monitor your kids' social media use. They won't like it, but you have to be the parent first and the friend later. When my son set up his Facebook account, I got the password until he was off to college. He also was required to be my "friend" so that I could view his material. I never had to use the password once.
- Encourage your kids to share positive thoughts and experiences and help them understand how to do it in a humble way. Posts such as "I got to work at the Make-A-Wish event tonight and it was really great" do the trick nicely. Posts like "Suzy is such a jerk" say something entirely different about the person posting.

CHAPTER NINE
MONEY ISN'T EVERYTHING, BUT IT'S REALLY IMPORTANT

"Money isn't the most important thing in life, but it's reasonably close to oxygen on the 'gotta have it' scale"
- Zig Ziglar, author and motivational speaker

I told you earlier that it is the relationships in your life that make you rich, not necessarily money. That is absolutely true, but there can be no doubt that money is important in our lives. We live in a society where you need money to buy the things you want and need. So, whether it is important to you or not, you need it. Some people are perfectly happy with a simple life, and they need less money than others. Other people have larger desires. The choice is, again, up to you. You choose what level of income you want to be at, and how hard you are willing to work to get it.

Self-induced Stress

There is no doubt that money is a major cause of stress in our lives. As the bills pile up or as you have to sit at home because you don't have money when your friends go out, money and stress go hand in hand. Many relationships and marriages fall apart because of money. I am always intrigued by how many celebrities or sports stars end up broke after having more money than most of us could ever imagine. The truth is that most of these money problems are self-induced. I have had plenty of stressful nights because I made the choice to buy something fun instead of paying a bill or taking care of something that was broken.

Knowing that money is one of the major stressors in

life should motivate us to try and avoid the pitfalls. It often doesn't. Like everything else in this book, sound money management is a matter of choice, priorities, and self-discipline. You have to be able to give up some instant gratification for long term piece of mind.

A Simple Equation

The first principle of sound money management is a simple equation. The amount you spend has to be less than or equal to the amount you earn. That's where a lot of people get into trouble. Often, once you are in financial trouble, it is very difficult to get out.

Save, Save, Save

In the perfect world, the amount you spend should absolutely be less than the amount you earn, so that you can save money. Save money for a rainy day, save money for a big thing down the road, or save money for retirement. That's why this section has three saves in the title, because there are three reasons for you to save. If you save, you will absolutely have some measure of peace of mind. Even if you never need the rainy day fund, meaning that nothing huge ever goes wrong in your life, you can later put that into your retirement savings and enjoy more after your days of working are done.

Saving for a rainy day is not much fun. It is disturbing to think that we have to put money away for catastrophe. Sadly, it is true. Catastrophes can come dressed as any number of things. They can be sickness or the loss of a job. They can be a natural disaster or tragedy that forces you from your home. Hurricane Katrina, the terrible tornadoes that devastate the Midwest every year, or Super Storm Sandy are all examples of this. They can be the failure of something expensive in your house like a furnace or a roof. Worse yet, they can be the sudden death of a loved one who contributed to the household income. Any one of those things can cause a serious financial strain on you. Well run businesses even put money aside for bad times, as being able to weather a storm is crucial to long-term success.

Saving for something big is also a really good plan. The two things that almost all of us will have to use credit for are buying a house and buying a car. Both of those turn into pretty major monthly expenses. You can lower those monthly payments by paying a portion of the total cost up front in the form of a down payment. In terms of a house, it also means that right away you have some equity, or value which is yours and not the bank's.

When we bought our first house, we were still trying to clean up the financial disaster related to our daughter's death. We didn't have any money to put down on the house. As a matter of fact, we even mortgaged all of the attorney's fees and other related costs along with the price of the house. The result was that we took a mortgage for $114,000 on a house for which we only paid $109,000. Our monthly mortgage payment was higher and because we had no money to put down, we looked like a credit risk, so we also paid a slightly higher interest rate. Had we been able to put 10-20% down on the house, we would have looked more responsible in the eyes of the lender and gotten a lower rate, as well as lowered our monthly payments.

I mentioned a house and a car, but there are many other things for which you should save, as well. I am fundamentally against using credit to buy things we don't need. When we went on a cruise, we paid cash for most of it. We saved money for months and used our credit cards for only a few things. Vacations are great. I love to spend money on things that create memories. I don't love to keep paying for them, with interest, for a year or more after we have returned. I want the memories to be of the beaches and the sunsets, not of the painful payments. My rule is that we plan in advance and save money for the vacation, not put it on the credit card. Even when I have to use a credit card to reserve a hotel room or a car, I often pay cash when it is time to check-out.

Toys are another thing for which I try not to pay interest. When I want a new toy, like a TV, laptop, or hot tub, I save my money until I have enough to buy it. You would be surprised how quickly you can save money for something you really want.

The final, and, arguably, most important, thing you need to save for is your retirement. Young people often laugh when I ask if them if they have a retirement account. They are 18, 19, 20 years old. In most cases, they haven't even found their first real job yet and I am asking them to think about retirement. When you are young is the best time to think about retirement.

Let's say, for example, that you need a million dollars to retire comfortably. Let's also say that you want to retire at age 65. If you wait until you are 40 to start thinking about it, like I did, it means that you either have to put $40,000 per year away, or you have to work a lot longer to reach your goal. If you start to think about retirement ten years earlier, at age 30, you have to put away around $28,000 a year. If you start thinking about it at age 18, you have to put away around $21,000 a year.

I know what you are saying. "Woah, I can't afford to put away $21,000 per year." That is absolutely true. Some entry level jobs only pay $21,000 per year, and certainly you can't put away all of your income. Remember, this is an average per year. Early in your life you will put away considerably less money than you will put away later in your life. The second thing to remember is that you need to get in the habit of saving for retirement. The earlier you start, the more likely you will be successful. If you shoot for a million dollars and end up with a half a million, you are still better off than you were before. Finally, there are some tools to help you grow your retirement money. Those numbers I gave you earlier didn't include your account gaining any interest.

Retirement savings accounts are a special kind of

account. They are designed, by nature, to be a long-term savings vehicle. Because you agree to tie up your money for a long period of time, you receive a higher interest rate. Here's an example. Let's say you can only put $100 in your retirement savings account this year. If it gains 2% interest, you will have $102 in the account at the end of the year. Now the account will gain interest on that additional $2, which is money that you never put in there. If you put the same $100 in the account the following year, it will be worth $206 at the end of the year. If you only put $100 a year for 10 years, the account will be worth $1117. So, you made $117 or 11.7% on that money over ten years.

The above example shows how you can get your money to grow without doing much. The interest paid for you to tie up your money even gets paid on the money that you didn't put in there. This example is very small, and it also assumes that you never increase your annual contribution to your account. As your pay increases each year, you should increase the amount you put away. Let's say you increase the amount you contribute each year by only $10. So the first year is $100, the second is $110 and so on. Over the same 10 years that account would be worth $1601. Slowly but surely, through a combination of your increased contributions and interest compounding on your money, you will grow a nice account that you can retire on.

Another great tool for saving for retirement is an account that is managed by your employer. Many employers offer a retirement program called a 401(k). What makes this better is that for every dollar you put in, your employer will often match a certain percentage of that. So, if you put in $100 a year and your employer matches 50%, you will have $150 at the end of the year, even though you contributed the same amount. There are limits on how much the employer will contribute. This grows your money even faster.

Both of these retirement tools require one thing from you. Sacrifice. You have to put money into them in order for them to grow. That means you have to give up something now, and you won't see the reward until many years in the future.

The good news is that the banks and your employers have teamed up to make this easier for you. Direct deposit allows for money from your paycheck to be deposited into a number of different accounts, or different banks. By the time I see my paycheck each week, money has already been deposited into my retirement account and a couple of different savings accounts, so that I don't even have to think about it. My money is growing and I don't have to do a thing.

There are all sorts of different savings products available to you. The longer you agree to leave your money in the bank, the higher the interest rate the banks will pay you. There are also different investment opportunities like stocks and mutual funds. These are also ways to grow your money without you having to physically work for that money. It is always a great idea to have your money making more money for you while it is sitting there waiting for you to use it.

For his 16th birthday, I gave my son $250. I put $200 in a savings account and $50 in a checking account and told him he was only allowed to spend the $50. We also made the rule that every time he made a deposit, he had to put something in each account. He has a nice habit of saving now and his money is growing.

The most important lesson here, however, is that you need to save money, and it is never too early to start thinking about these issues. Get in the habit of responsible money management at an early age.

Credit

I have to tell you, I am not a big fan of credit. I try to use it as sparingly as possible. Why? Because I used it a lot when I was younger and it got me in trouble.

As I said earlier, there are times where the use of credit is necessary. It is hard to imagine too many people having $150,000 in cash laying around to buy a house. Cars are also expensive enough that it is difficult to pay cash for them, unless you are buying an older used car. In those cases, it is absolutely necessary to use credit. In other cases, you should try to buy as many things as possible with cash.

Another form of credit you might not be able to avoid in life is student loans. We have already talked about the astronomical cost of college, so student loans will most likely be necessary. The problem with student loans is that they are generally large sums of money, so they take many years to pay off. They are also government backed loans, so if you find yourself in financial trouble, they are not dischargeable in bankruptcy. The most important thing to do is to understand your loans before you take them. American Student Assistance, a private, not-for-profit organization has set up a nice website at asa.org that is full of information about student loans. Spend some time reviewing the site so that you can make good decisions before taking loans, and also to understand your rights in regards to student loans.

Credit cards are a great tool. They allow us to buy things now and pay for them later, or even break up the large price into smaller payments. The problem with credit cards is that like everything else, they have a price. The bank will loan you the money for your purchase, but you have to pay them back with interest. In recent years, those interest rates have skyrocketed and banks have put extremely high fees on the credit cards for late payments or for going over your limit. The high interest rates and the high fees can both spell big trouble for credit users, particularly young ones who don't understand how they add a lot to your monthly bill.

The interest on a credit card balance works just like the interest on those savings accounts we just talked about. It grows on the money that you owe the bank. The difference?

The banks give you very low interest rates on your savings accounts. On the other hand, they charge very high interest rates on the money that you borrow on credit cards. By high, I mean 19-29%. That means for every dollar you borrow, you are going to pay $1.19-$1.29 back. If you don't pay the whole thing back at the same time, then the interest grows on the money you carry over. If you are late on a payment, they throw a $25 or $30 late fee at you and then the interest starts to grow on that late fee as well. It is very easy to find yourself underwater and unable to meet your credit card payments. If you only pay back the minimum payment listed on your credit card bill, it could be years and years before you actually pay it off.

In 2009 Congress passed the Credit CARD Act, and one provision of the law required banks to include on the monthly bill a warning that showed how long it would take to pay off the entire balance if the cardholder only paid the minimum payment. It also must tell you approximately how much you will pay back. Here is an example from an actual credit card bill.

Total balance due: $1583.21
Annual Percentage Rate (APR) of interest: 29.99%
Minimum payment: $56.00

If you make no more additional charges using this card and each month you pay	You will pay off the balance shown on this statement in about	And you will end up paying an estimated total of
Only the minimum payment	11 years	$4396
$68.00	3 years	$2341 (savings $1965)

That's quite a difference in both length of time to pay back and in total paid to the bank by just raising your payment $12.00 per month.

In my opinion, the individual store branded credit cards are the worst. They use offers of getting an additional 10%- 20% off the price in order to entice you to use them. Why would they do that? Because if they give you 15% off and charge you 25% interest, it means that they are actually making an additional 10% over the price of what a customer who uses cash pays. Please remember that they wouldn't offer it if they couldn't make money.

Remember, credit cards are generally a very bad deal for the consumer. It's like gambling in a big casino. The odds always favor the house, not the player. The same is true of credit cards.

Credit Scores

I'm sure that you've all seen the TV commercials advertising companies where you can see your credit scores. A credit score is a rating that you are given which tells potential lenders whether you are a good or bad credit risk. The lenders view these credit scores before deciding whether they will give you a loan or a credit card. The higher your credit score, the more likely you are to get a loan. Also, if you have an excellent score, you might enjoy much lower interest rates on the loans or credit cards that you are offered.

There are several different agencies that rate your credit score. In the simplest terms, your score depends on your payment history, how much credit you already have, and how much money you owe. If you owe a lower amount of money and you always pay on time, you are going to have a very high credit score. If you run your credit cards up near their maximum limits or have a variety of outstanding loans, and you make late payments, your credit score will be much lower.

Your credit score is another very important part of your image. Not only will it determine whether or not you get loans for important things like cars and houses, but nowadays some employers check your credit worthiness before they hire you. It is perceived that people who have bad credit often have other problems on the job that employers aren't willing to deal with. While a credit report doesn't reflect the circumstances that may have put a person in bad credit standing, employers may see it is an indication of a potential employee's character. If they see the poor credit as a reflection of the job candidate's organizational skills and self-discipline, that candidate may not get hired for the job.

The credit system definitely does not operate in your favor. It is easy to get behind and extremely hard to get out from under heavy debt. The only way that you can win at credit is if you use your credit card and pay off the entire balance every month. Then you can collect whatever reward points or cash back that the bank offers, and pay no interest or late fees. Be very careful with how you use credit.

Be Responsible

Every month I get a stack of bills. My mortgage, my car payment, various types of insurance and all of my utility payments are monthly obligations that I have. It used to be that I had to sit down and write checks and mail payments to the different businesses to which I owed money. Things have changed drastically in the last decade. The advent of technology, specifically the Internet, has made it so much easier to pay our bills. Most of my bills don't even come in the mail anymore. I get e-bills sent directly to my e-mail account. I can usually go online and with a few clicks my bill is paid.

One of the coolest inventions is the automatic payment. Several of the businesses to which I owe money automatically deduct the amount I owe directly from my bank account. It is like magic and I never really have to think about it. Our mortgage payment, car payment, auto insurance payment, and life-insurance payment are all scheduled to be withdrawn automatically from our bank account on a scheduled day each month. All we have to do is make sure the money is in the bank account on the scheduled day. Bada-bing bada-boom, bill paid. Those are all of the most important bills. We don't do it with every bill because we might need flexibility in exactly when we pay the others. Also, most of the other bills change in amount from month to month, and so I want to be aware of those bills. If they are automatic, I tend to pay less attention to them.

Here's a few tips for responsible money management;

- Pay yourself first. Make sure that money goes into each of your savings accounts before you pay attention to the other things. Even give yourself a weekly allowance for entertainment and fun. It might mean that you have to save for a short period of time to buy that new coat or go on a date to the expensive restaurant, but it'll be worth it in the long run.

- Use direct deposit to put money into your savings and retirement before you ever see your paycheck. You'll be tricking yourself into thinking that the only money you have is the money you see, while your savings grow.

- Pay your debts on time. Your credit score can be of real benefit, or it can be a boulder that you have to carry around on your back everywhere you go. Use automatic deductions to pay your bills, then you don't even have to think about it.

- Use credit sparingly. The rules and interest rates are designed to make sure that the lenders make money, a lot of it. If they are making a lot, it means that you are paying a lot. Save the money in advance and then pay cash for things that you don't need. Only use credit when absolutely necessary. It might mean you have to sacrifice.

- Setting your priorities and self-discipline are the keys to good money management.

Who's The Boss?

One of the next big questions is who are you going to work for? There are many potential answers to that question. The first is that you can go to college and work hard and get a job with a big company. A large company is defined by the United States Small Business Administration (SBA) as any business that has more than 500 employees. In addition to your paycheck, you might get a standard benefits package that includes sick days and retirement and some portion of your health insurance paid for. Depending on the size of the company, you'll certainly have your own supervisor, but you may never even meet the person at the top. Again, depending on the size of the business, you may or may not have room to advance in the company. In a large corporation, there is usually room for advancement, but there is also a lot of competition for those promotions. You really have to shine, and sometimes the environment can be very cut-throat.

The second option is working for a small business. According to the SBA website (sba.gov), there were approximately 6 million small businesses in the United States in 2010 that employed people. These 6 million employers accounted for just under 50% of the total private sector jobs in America. These are smaller companies where often the founder and/or a family are running the business. You are much more likely to be able to interact with the top levels of the company in small businesses. Because of that, you may be included in company decision making. Many of these businesses have excellent ties to the communities in which they were founded in. Many of them also offer good pay and benefits.

The third choice is working for yourself. The same SBA webpage estimates that there are over 20 million self-employed people in this country right now. Whether they are electricians or plumbers in the service industry, or consultants to other businesses, these are people who work by themselves every single day. This sector includes artists, photographers, authors, and musicians. Even doctors and lawyers sometimes set up their own shop and go it alone.

The interesting thing is that we seldom talk about this idea of working for yourself in the high school or even the college setting. Our current educational system, it seems, is definitely skewed towards the idea of training you to go work for someone else.

The truth of the matter is that small business and entrepreneurs make up a huge part of the modern American workforce. Small firms account for 99.7% of all U.S. employers. Innovation by small business is one of the very foundations upon which the United States economy is built, and the idea goes largely ignored in our schools.

There are a couple of things that you should know before you run off and start your own business. First, it's hard work. When you own the business, you are ultimately responsible for every single thing. That means you have to find the customers, sell them on hiring you, do the work, and send out the invoices to get paid. You have to balance the checkbook and pay the bills. You have to order the supplies, and clean the office, including the bathrooms. The problem that most small business owners have is that of all of those tasks I just mentioned, only one of them actually produces any income for which you can bill people. That's the "do the work" step. All of the rest needs to be done, but you can't charge anyone for it. It is hard work.

There are plenty of benefits to working for yourself. You get to set your own rules, and your own hours (it is almost 8pm at night while I am typing this) and you get to set your own dress code. Bestselling author and personal success coach, Carrie Wilkerson, named her book and her brand "The Barefoot Executive". She works from home and she can get comfortable without shoes while doing lots of her work. You get to take lunch when you want to, and so long as the work is done, you can knock off early to go watch your sister or your daughter accept an award at school. Assuming that you are working hard and making money, you can set your own prices and you can accept or turn down whatever work you choose. I have turned down jobs because I know the person is too difficult to work with. In a big company they will accept the work and assign someone lower down the chain to deal with the difficult customer. While there are a lot of benefits to working for yourself, it is very hard work.

Earlier in the book I mentioned Steve Jobs and Steve Wozniak, the co-founders of Apple Computer. These two guys started Apple computer in 1976 by putting together computer kits that Wozniak made by hand. In 2012, after quite a ride, Apple Computer became the most valuable technology company in history.

Bill Hewlett and Dave Packard started the computer giant Hewlett Packard or HP in 1939 in their garage, making electrical test instruments. Eventually they became the industry leader in computer printers.

Debbi Fields had a great recipe for chocolate chip cookies and she wanted to share it. She convinced the bank to loan her money to open a bakery. Now Mrs. Fields Cookies has over 600 locations in the US and 10 other countries.

The list of entrepreneurs is long and it includes some of my heroes: Steve Case (AOL), Oprah Winphrey, Henry Ford, Thomas Edison, Jeff Bezos (Amazon), and Mary Kay Ash (Mary Kay Cosmetics). These are all people who had an idea they believed in and weren't afraid to take on the risk and responsibility of working for themselves.

Entrepreneurial Spirit

Do you have the drive to make money by yourself? Do you have good ideas for new products? Do you look at processes and try to find better ways to do things? Do you like to help people with your knowledge or contacts? If the answer is yes to any or all of those, it sounds like you have the entrepreneurial spirit. Now the only question is how badly you want to succeed at your own business.

Starting a Business Isn't Hard

The actual process of starting a business is quite easy and not very expensive. You can file a certificate to be a "sole proprietorship" at your county hall and be doing business that same day under your new business name. In my home state of New York, the cost of that is under $50. There are other things you will need, like a bank account and a way for people to contact you, maybe your cell phone is just fine for this, but you can see that for this form of business, it is easy and inexpensive to get going. I have been operating as a sole proprietorship since 1992, and it has suited me just fine.

If you are doing work that has a higher risk of damage or injury, you will want to protect yourself and your personal assets by setting up your business as a corporation. This way, if you accidently injure someone or cause property damage, the person can only sue you for the value of the assets of the corporation, not for all of your personal assets. This filing is more expensive, and takes more time to accomplish, but it is essential to protect yourself and your family in the event of mishap.

There are multiple types of corporations that can be formed: general corporations, close corporations, limited liability corporations (LLC), and S corporations, each of which has its own advantages and disadvantages. The biggest differences between them tend to involve the number of stockholders and how the corporation and its stockholders pay taxes. If you are going to go the route of a corporation it is best to consult an attorney and/or accountant on which corporate structure is best for what you want to do.

Where's The Money?

The financing for your business can come in a variety of different forms. You can finance it yourself, which is often the best way. In this model you have no one to answer to but yourself. As you involve more people in the process, you will have more opinions and you will also have more restrictions placed on you by the people or the banks who want to make sure their investment is safe. If you are going to look for outside financing, there are a few different options.

The Small Business Administration (www.sba.gov) has a host of lower interest loan programs available for start up businesses. These programs are designed to help seed start-up companies or even to help established companies fund expansions. Local banks offer loans to small businesses as well. When you take out these loans, you make monthly payments just like a car loan or a home mortgage.

Seeking investors is another route to funding your business endeavor. This, however, is generally the most intrusive. When you take on investors, you have to give up a percentage of your company. This doesn't only represent giving up a percentage of profits, but also a percentage of control. When you take on investors you often will no longer be able to make 100% of the decisions in your company.

Remember that professional investors are generally successful business people. They became successful and believe in the practices that made them successful. In order for them to give you money, they often want you to use their practices in the daily operation of your business. You have to clearly weigh the need for money versus the need for you to maintain control. Remember that the only reason a professional investor would invest in you is that they see an opportunity to make money. They are not necessarily passionate about the idea, as you are, and that can cause friction. On the other hand, they can bring experience and expertise that you may not have, giving you more tools for achieving success. As I said earlier, everything has a price. You get money to start or grow your business, and they get some control over the decisions being made.

What's The Business For You?

There are all sorts of business opportunities for you. As a matter of fact, there probably have never been more opportunities than there are now. Whether you start your own business or buy a franchise of an existing, established brand name business, the choices are endless. Here's a list of different possibilities for you.

Service businesses – What can you do for people and get paid for it? This is the landscaping, plumbing, and carpentry business. If you are an artist or a musician, you fit in here too. Maybe you can paint murals on children's bedroom walls or take photos at weddings. What talent or skill do you have that you can turn into money?

Product based businesses – This is two-fold. Maybe you have created a new tool or new device that makes your job easier. Can you manufacture this new product and sell it to the masses for a profit? On the other hand, maybe you are just a really great salesperson and you make a deal with other manufacturers and go out and sell their product. In either case, your earnings are based on the number of units of the product that you sell.

Knowledge based business – What expertise do you have that people will pay you to teach them? Can you coach people to get better at something and have them pay you for it? There are coaches for everything these days. There are business coaches, life coaches, public speaking coaches, beauty pageant coaches, and the list goes on and on. Do you have a real knack for something, or some experiences that you could turn into a successful coaching or consulting business? This is a great business opportunity because it usually comes with very little overhead. It is also great because with today's technology you can do your coaching over the phone or over the internet to people all over the world.

Information based business – This is similar to the knowledge based business, in that you are selling your knowledge or experience. The difference is that this is not a one on one or even small group endeavor. It involves taking your knowledge or your story and putting it into a book or into a video and selling it. This is another industry that has benefitted dramatically with the explosion of the internet. In the old days you had to write the book and find a publisher. Nowadays with self-publishing, and even e-books, everyone has great access to getting their words in print. Even distribution is cheaper with technology. I believe every single person has a story that is interesting. What is your accomplishment that will interest people? The market is huge and so is the potential. Tell your story. There are plenty of people who will pay to hear it

Real estate business – While this isn't my thing, there is always potential in real estate. Even in a down market, property values are low and there are a lot of foreclosed properties selling at rock bottom prices. You can buy houses cheaply and then rent them out or find properties that need work and flip them over at decent profits. These are areas where each transaction can yield much larger profits. If you can average $10,000 or more in profit per property, it doesn't take many sales in a year to make a decent living. You just need to know how to research and find those low priced properties.

Starting your own business can be one of the most challenging, but most rewarding endeavors you ever undertake. If you play your cards right, there are so many benefits. Some of these opportunities require some money to get them started, while others just require your time and energy.

When I was growing up, I received a weekly allowance for doing my set of chores. If I wanted more money, my dad would give me other jobs to do to earn it. I was often out washing the car on a Saturday to earn an extra buck or two. I had my own newspaper delivery route when I was a kid. The lessons I learned were good ones, and they have served me through my whole life. There are so many ways to make money in this world, no matter what age you are. If you want money, go get it. Ask the neighbors down the street if you can shovel their driveway or mow their lawn. If you like to shop, see if there are people who don't like it and who would pay you to do it for them. If you are smart and use coupons for all of your customers, it really won't even cost them more than if they shopped themselves. That's a win for both of you.

Use technology to make money, sell the things in your basement, or market your goods or services on social media or any one of the great internet selling sites. There are vast amounts of money to be made on the internet these days. All you have to do is dedicate yourself to the process.

Chapter Nine Highlights

- One of the biggest sources of stress in our life is money.
- The amount you spend needs to be less than or equal to the amount you earn.
- Save, save, save, for rainy days, the next big thing or retirement.
- The longer you save the less you need to sacrifice each week or month.
- Use credit sparingly. It is so easy to find yourself in trouble with high interest rate loans and credit cards.
- Your credit score can be a great benefit or a boulder on your back.
- Pay your bills on time.
- Starting your own business is not terribly difficult.
- There are a variety of ways to fund a new business.
- There are many different ways to make money these days.

- The explosion of technology has really made it much easier to do business.

ACTIVITIES

Student Activities

- Start to save money right now. Even if it is just a jar on your dresser. Every single time you get some money through a paycheck or a gift, put a little in your savings. Get in the habit of saving.
- Begin to think about retirement now. Start saving for it now, even if it is a very small amount. The longer you save, the more money you will have for comfortable retirement. No money that goes into this fund should ever come out until it is time to retire.

Teacher activities

- Talk about our nation's greatest entrepreneurs, particularly the new ones. When a guy like Mark Zuckerberg makes billions of dollars before he is 30 years old, that is inspiring.

Parent Activities

- If you don't already have it, take your child and set up a checking and savings account for them. Set up rules where they have to deposit into both accounts.
- Talk about money with your kids. The more they know, the better equipped they will be. If you have a retirement account, show them the statements from time to time so that they can see the money grow. Now that's inspiring.

CHAPTER TEN
TAKE CARE OF YOU

"When you care for one aspect of your human form, you cannot help but care for all of them. A healthy mind creates a healthy spirit; a healthy spirit thrives best in a healthy body. Truly feeling good is only possible when all the parts are working well."
- Kate Sciandra, author

This chapter title might sound pretty obvious. Of course you are going to take care of you. What it isn't necessarily obvious, is what exactly is involved with taking care of you. I think most of us agree that walking into the path of an oncoming bus would be detrimental to our well being. We don't necessarily feel the same about smoking, eating poorly, or not exercising.

Many of us seldom take time to pay attention and tend to our whole selves. There are three essential states of well-being - the intellectual, the physical, and the emotional sides of our life. Each of those states has very real needs and will thrive if well fed. Most of us have a tendency to go through life reacting to the stimulus around us, instead of controlling which stimulus we allow into our lives.

The most important thing to consider is that you have to actively look for ways to take care of yourself, and you should never expect anyone but yourself to do this.

Before I became a teacher, I worked for a big box home improvement retailer, and we had a great company mission that we tried to honor always, the philosophy of "continuous improvement". We knew we were pretty darn good at certain things. Our stores were beautiful, bright, and clean, and our customer service was top-notch. Knowing that we were better than our competition in those areas, It would have been easy to sit back and accept that we were the best. We didn't. "Continuous improvement" meant that no matter how good we were at something, we would always work to get better. Almost two decades after I left that company, "continuous improvement" remains one of my core values. I am always looking for ways to get better at what I do.

> *"The road to success is always under construction."*
>
> *– James C. Miller, United States politician and economist*

In 2014 I celebrated 15 years of teaching the Public Speaking class at my school. In 2010 I taught a curriculum that I was very comfortable with, and one that I knew well. That year, I was introduced to TED Talks vidoes, and I was completely blown away. After watching a few of the TED presentations, I realized that I was doing it all wrong. I was teaching public speaking from an old school point of view. The world had changed drastically in the past 5-10 years, but my curriculum had not. I rewrote the whole curriculum, using modern ideas and technology and it has really paid off. I believe my students are enjoying the course more, and they are definitely producing better speeches.

The point is, don't accept the status quo. Learn new things, do new things and find healthy ways to live your life that will expand not only the quantity of your life, but the quality.

Learning Doesn't End With A Diploma

Just like everything else in this book, feeding your intellectual well-being is a choice. I have been a teacher for almost 20 years and I cannot tell you how often I hear kids say that they can't wait to finish school and quit learning all of the useless stuff. If I had a nickel for every time anyone ever asked me when they would use math or science in the real world, I could retire right now.

I am sure you have heard the old adage that life is a journey and the way to make the most of it is to continue to learn new things every day. Learning something every day doesn't mean that you have to learn a new way to factor equations, or split the atom; focus on things that interest you. Maybe learn new ways to cook, or take photographs in low light, or teach yourself to juggle. With all of the information on the Internet, there is no excuse not to find the answers to your questions. As far as learning to do something you've never done before, ask around; you'll be surprised at what the people around you know how to do. And remember, there is a video on the internet for almost everything.

As I mentioned, I watch a lot of TED Talk videos. There are so many topics and so many videos available. They are, at most, only 18 minutes long. I can watch that while I am on the treadmill or on my lunch period. I can watch them after dinner or first thing in the morning. I learn so much from them.

I used to limit myself in my reading. I would read one book, and when I was finished, I would start another. A few years ago, my friend and co-worker, Jamie Holden told me that he had a book that he keeps at school to read and a book that he reads at home. I said, "I couldn't do that. It would confuse me." His response changed my reading life. He said, "You watch more than one TV show per season." He was right. As soon as I start watching a new episode, I am reminded of the last one. Nowadays I have 2 or 3 books going at a time. I read fiction the last few minutes of everyday. It helps to clear my mind. During the day, however, I read books on leadership, public speaking, social media, education, and politics, all of the things that I love and that I can bring to my lessons at school.

Whether it is books, magazines, or the web, you have to continually feed your mind so that it stays sharp and engaged. Who knows what inspiration you will find in the most unlikely places. Set aside some time each week to feed your mind good things and keep it working well by finding problems to solve, like crossword puzzles, Sudoku, or puzzle games on the Internet. If you don't use a tool it becomes rusty from lack of use. Your mind is no different. Engage on a path that helps you continually improve your mind.

Your Body Is A Temple

Singer Jimmy Buffett has a great line in the song "Fruitcakes". He sings, "I treat my body like a temple, you treat yours like a tent." I am not going to lie, when it comes to my physical well-being, I have spent most of my life in the tent, not the temple.

I was a mediocre athlete, who stopped playing school soccer after 9th grade. In college I played some intramurals and then I played a little softball for a few years. After that I was done, and I was never one for exercise.

For most of my life, I was very thin. I was about 150 pounds the day I got married in 1988. As a guy who is 6'-1" that was too thin. I married a great cook and she has done her job......too well. I am now north of 200 pounds. Come on, I live in Buffalo, chicken wings are a staple food for me.

If I had one do-over, I wish that I had incorporated exercise more fully into my life, but because I didn't, it is now a struggle.

Over the past decade I developed my family tradition of high blood pressure. Every single time that I visit my doctor he tells me that losing weight will lower my blood pressure. I know from reading and TV that even 20-30 minutes of walking a day will have a dramatic effect on my overall health. The truth is, I am much better about it when it is nice outside and I can take a walk in the park. When I do regular exercise, I feel better, I sleep better, and I have a lot more energy. Those are three pretty good reasons to exercise.

Here's how I try to look at it now. It's like mowing the lawn. I wouldn't say that I like any part of mowing the lawn, but it has to be done, so I do it. There is no point in being miserable about it.

Another thing that happens as you age is that you tend to get stiffer. Even a short daily stretching session will help you keep your muscles from tightening up and will keep you a little more flexible and relieve pain in your life. If you want more flexibility, enroll in a yoga class. What is the first thing your dog or cat does when they wake up? A quick stretch to get them going before they head off to find some trouble.

In addition to creating good exercise habits, what you eat is very important. This is definitely another area in which I have trouble. I hate to cook, and I like junk food and bacon and sausage and everything else that is bad for me. What I don't like a lot is vegetables, the food group that is overflowing with vitamins and minerals. One of my friends from high school, Sally Allgaier, is a gym owner and a competitive body builder in her late 40s. She says all the time "you can't exercise yourself out of a bad diet". Sally looks better than most people half her age, because she eats right and exercises regularly.

In recent years, we have really stepped up the national conversation about obesity. Sadly, one of the by-products of our high-tech society is that there are so many things to do in front of the TV or computer. When I was growing up, we played outside. We had pick-up games in the streets or on the front lawn of the school. My parents didn't let us sit around on a sunny day.

Here's the one thing I wish all kids, and parents would do. Think about creating a habit of exercise right now. If you do it while you are young, that habit will carry you through your life. But even if you are older, it is never too late to start. The best part about a habit of exercise is you can do it with other people. Taking a walk with your grandmother or your father will benefit you both. A walk on a beautiful day is great for clearing the mind. There is nothing like fresh air to get you feeling good. Also, the time you spend together will also feed your emotional well-being.

Getting Better All the Time

This is yet another choice that you can make in life. You can let yourself get weak or you can take a proactive approach to making yourself a little bit better each and every day. Think about a machine. If you run it for its intended purpose and you maintain it regularly and you put quality parts and oil into it, the machine will do its job optimally. If you neglect it, it will operate at a lower efficiency or it will break down all together. You should take care of your personal human machine, by keeping it moving and feeding it good things. While there is no guarantee that it will last a long time, there are definite and proven benefits to giving it your attention.

Emotions

Your emotional well-being comes from several different sources, and we have talked about many of them already. The most important element of your emotional well-being is relationships. These relationships can be with your family and friends, or they can include a spiritual relationship with a higher power. No matter who your strongest relationships are with, it is essential that you spend time tending to them, just as you spend time tending to our body and your intellect.

Tending to strong relationships sounds like work, but it certainly doesn't always have to be. Little things go a long way. Often, these little gestures can serve more than one purpose. Grandparents, for example, love to spend time with their grandchildren and great grandchildren. Taking them shopping or taking a walk with them might help you take care of other tasks that you need to do at the same time. At the end of your time together, I am sure you will see how much it meant to them. This is the stuff that feeds your emotional well-being.

If you are a spiritual person, daily reflection or prayer can feed your emotional well being, as it can provide cleansing moments. Most religions believe in recognizing and offering thanks for the wonderful things, the blessings that you have been given. We talked about the importance of genuine gratitude in chapter seven. That recognition and expression of gratitude will definitely feed your emotional well-being, whether you are religious or not. One of the greatest things about spirituality is the acknowledgement that there is something bigger than you.

There is more and more proof that mindfulness, meditation, and yoga also provide great benefits to your quality of life. They are proven methods of stress relief and can have big effects on your health and your mood.

We talked already about volunteerism. There is no doubt that serving the community around you will feed your emotional well-being. The feeling of accomplishment is very strong when you offer your time, expertise, or money to benefit people who are less fortunate than you. No one appreciates your time more than children. Be a regular mentor to someone younger than yourself, and see how that feeds your emotional well being. That includes being a coach, directing plays, or being a scout leader. Kids benefit from your attention and you benefit from their appreciation. If you are a kid now, there are always younger kids out there that are looking for someone to look up to. Be that role model.

You have three different states of well-being, and it is important to not only acknowledge them, but also to actively choose activities that will tend to each of them. Each of these areas is distinctly different and requires very different activities to feed them. Like a financial investment, the reward is not often immediate, but tending to your different states of well-being is a long term investment that will pay dividends your whole life. And like a good financial portfolio, it is best to look for activities in your life that provide a nice balance. All three of your states of well-being need equal time.

Chapter Ten Highlights

- You have three different states of well-being, the intellectual, the physical and the emotional.
- Each different state has very different needs.
- We should all embrace a life that is based on the premise that no matter how good we are, we can continuously find ways to improve ourselves.

ACTIVITIES

Student Activities

- Read things that aren't school or work related for at least 15-20 minutes a day. It doesn't matter whether it is the sports page, a blog, or some fiction. Read, read, read.
- Find time to exercise. Make sure you are working to create the life-long habit of daily exercise. Keep on exercising during your extended breaks from school.
- Eat healthy. This is a choice.

Teacher Activities

- Tell the kids about interesting things that you do to contribute to your well-being. Did you run in a 5K race, or maybe even a marathon? Tell them about it.
- Tell the kids a new "cool" fact every day. There are always fun things that relate to every content area.
- Share your professional development experiences with the kids. I always try to tell them what I learned when I get back from a conference or professional development day.

Parent Activities

- Do things together that contribute to your states of well-being. Family time together builds a strong family well into the future, and there is nothing that contributes to well-being more than that.
- You typically control the menu in the house. Make sure everyone is eating healthy.
- Exercise together. Walks or bike rides are healthy and create great bonding time.

CONCLUSION

"You may delay, but time will not."
– Benjamin Franklin, Founding Father

We've come to the end. There are certainly a lot more ideas to help you achieve success that I could share here, but, in my opinion, these are the most important. They are the ones that support you on the way to incredible personal success. Now, the question to you is, what are you waiting for? You need to get started today.

If you learned nothing else from this book, I am hoping that this one thing bubbled to the top. I used the word "choice" or one of its derivatives 146 times in this book. There is no greater lesson that you can learn, in high school, college, or in life than that you do not have to accept any of your circumstances in life. You have the unique gift of being aware that if you dislike your current situation, then you also have the ability to choose to change it. Some changes are easier than others, but all begin with the *choice* to make that change.

Change is not easy. For whatever reason, most of us seem to be programmed to stick with the status quo, even if we dislike it. Perhaps it is because we fear what we do not know. Someone can tell us things will be better if we change, but uncertainty can keep us from moving forward. So, we settle for inactivity, even if it means staying in a situation that makes us uncomfortable. Like the Chinese philosopher, Lao Tzu said, "The journey of a thousand miles begins with a single step". The single step he talks about is the CHOICE to make a change. It can be the hardest step to take, but it is the most necessary. Nothing else is possible without that initial choice.

Once you've made the choice, you can use some of the other tools in this book to realize your dreams. You can create those habits that support all of your goals. It took the habit of thinking about this book every single day for me to get it done. Habits are so powerful, and so easy to create. You don't need an advanced education or any special skills. You just need to have the self-discipline to do it over and over again until you no longer have to think about it.

You have the unique ability to really see yourself. Use that self-awareness to define who you are. Use it to choose what is important to you. Once you decide what your values are, you can define the rest of your life around those values. It is easier to make decisions if you use your values as a compass, and to have that measuring post by which to evaluate your decisions. Your values are your map. Be aware of them and use them to steer you through the difficult times.

Remember, it is not the material stuff you gather along the way that makes you happy; it is the relationships you forge. Play an active role in all of the relationships that are important to you, don't wait for them to come to you. This life is too short and too unpredictable. If you wait to be involved with people you love, they may not be available when the time comes. So many people I know are sad that they didn't nurture and grow relationships when they had the opportunity.

Take some time to get to know yourself. You are the most important person in your life. That doesn't mean you should be selfish, but you should be aware of your wants and needs. Only you know what you are thinking, or what you need.

Develop a life that allows you to be happy and be proud of yourself in a humble way. Don't try to be perfect, because that isn't going to happen. Make your mistakes, learn from them, and then forgive yourself and get past them. Let me repeat that. Learn from your mistakes, and forgive yourself. If you do this, you won't be destined to make them over and over again. It's OK to learn from other people's mistakes, as well. It actually takes a lot of pressure off of you.

Another key to a good life is to like yourself. If you don't, identify what you don't like and change it. Everything is a choice.

See the things that you want in your mind. Visualize them, and visualize yourself enjoying the fruits of your achievements. Visualize them over and over again until suddenly you find that you have crossed the finish line, and you have what you want. Look to the future, and set very specific goals for yourself.

Remember that everything has a price, and be willing to sacrifice and pay the price for the things you really want in life. You really will appreciate things more if you had to work hard to get them. You will take pride in a job well done.

None of this is possible unless you feed your states of well-being. Each of the three, intellectual, physical, and emotional, has specific needs and deserves regular attention. They are like plants. If you feed and water them and give them the light they need, they will flourish. Since they are the individual elements that make up you, if they flourish, you flourish. This is habit is a worthwhile investment that will pay dividends throughout your whole life.

Life itself is a journey. Whenever we take a trip where there is a long drive involved, we try to find new and interesting places or places that we know that we already enjoy to stop at along the way. If all of your attention is set on getting to the destination and you don't enjoy the trip, you are missing some great opportunities. Who knows what great adventures lay around the next corner? Keep your eyes open, you won't see them if you aren't looking. And remember the destination is actually just a part of the journey. Find ways to enjoy the time you spend getting to your destination as well.

Finally, this is the most important part. At the end of

the day, the only thing holding you back is you. If you are willing to make the choice and pay the price, then you will achieve the greatness that you want, and that you deserve. What are you waiting for? Get out there and get started.

ACTIVITIES

Student Activities

- It's your future, not your parent's and not your teacher's. Make the choice to do at least 2 things per day that will move you closer to your vision of happiness and success.

Teacher Activities

- Lead by example always. Kids often have no more powerful role models in their lives than their teachers. Show them great behavior to model.
- Share your experiences. That's how kids learn from their role models. It's also how kids connect with their role models, by being inspired by them.

Parent Activities

- Encourage, encourage, encourage.
- Be active in your kids' lives. Before you know it, they will be off in college and then on to bigger and better things. If you want them to stay involved in your life, be involved in theirs, so you show them how important a strong family unit is.

ABOUT THE AUTHOR

Pete Herr never really knew he wanted to be a teacher until he woke one morning and realized he had spent almost a decade doing it. He took a roundabout way to the classroom which took him through jobs in professional theater, food service and corporate retail management, as well as owning his own small business for over 20 years.

During an almost two decade career he has been honored to be awarded "Teacher of the Year" on three different occasions; awards he holds very dear, as they all came from his students. When he is not teaching high school classes in Leadership, Marketing, Public Speaking, Personal Finance or Journalism, Pete enjoys connecting with his former students and continuing to help them learn.

A graduate of Wittenberg University, in Springfield, Ohio, Pete lives near Buffalo, NY with his wife, Linda; their son, Adam; and the puggle named Moxy.

CONNECT WITH PETE

Blog: peteherrsuccess.com

Twitter: twitter.com/peteherrsuccess

Facebook: facebook.com/peteherrsuccess